THANKS BE TO GOD!

MEMOIRS OF A PRACTICAL THEOLOGIAN

ROBERT BENNE

ALPB BOOKS
DELHI, NEW YORK

For with thee is the fountain of life;
In thy light do we see light.
Psalm 36: 9

2019 © ALPB Books
All rights reserved in the United States of America

ISBN 978-1-892921-39-0

American Lutheran Publicity Bureau
PO Box 327
Delhi, NY 13753

Robert Benne, *Thanks Be to God! Memoirs of a Practical Theologian*
(Delhi, NY: ALPB Books, 2019), 179 pp.

CONTENTS

Preface 9

Introduction 11

Chapter One Images 14
Chapter One
   Our Family–God's Greatest Earthly Gift 19
      Growing Up in West Point: 1937-1955 19
      College and Graduate School: 1955-1965 26
      Chicago Years: 1967-1982 27
      Salem Years: 1982- 29

Chapter Two Images 32
Chapter Two
   Inescapably Lutheran 37
      Early Years: 1937-1955 37
      Religious Life at Midland College: 1955-1959 42
      Religious Life in Germany: 1959-1960 47
      Religious Life in Graduate School: 1960-1965 48
      Religious Life at the Lutheran School
         of Theology at Chicago: 1965-1982 51
      Roanoke College and Salem, Virginia: 1982- 55

Chapter Three Images 64
Chapter Three
   Living the American Dream 69
      1937-1955 69
      1955-1959 77
      The Fulbright Year: 1959-1960 80

    Graduate School in the Period
        of Liberal Idealism: 1960-1965 82
    Teaching in Rock Island in the
        Old Augustana Seminary: 1965-1967 84
    Teaching at the Lutheran School
        of Theology: 1967-1982 86
    Teaching at Roanoke College: 1982-2012 91
    2012- 93

Chapter Four Images 96
Chapter Four
    My Calling as a Practical Theologian 101
    College and Graduate School: 1959-1965 102
    The Lutheran School of Theology
        at Chicago: 1967-1982 106
    Roanoke College: 1982- 120
        A Wake-Up Call 122
        Positive Steps 124
        Teaching and Writing in the 80s 125
        The Center for Religion and Society 127
        The Scholarly Reputation of the College 132
        The Mission and Identity of the College 134
        Further Writings 137
        Taking Up the Cause of
            Christian Higher Education 140
        A Painful Defeat 147
        Picking Up the Pieces 151
        Denouement 155
    The Era of Church Strife and New Beginnings 159
    Concluding Thoughts 168

Writings 173
    Books 173
    Chapters in Books 174

Index 177

For Joanna

Wife, Friend, Lover, Co-Parent, and Companion along Life's Way

PREFACE

You did not choose me, but I chose you and appointed you so that you might go and bear fruit. (John 15:16)

In my growing up years Mrs. Hasebroock was certainly the most distinguished woman in our town. She was president of the Nebraska Federation of Women's Clubs and later became president of the national organization. She was well-educated and had a fine voice, which she employed in the Grace Lutheran Church choir. She was married to the mayor of our town who was also our senator in the Nebraska Unicameral. They had a son, Robert, whom I idolized because he was a fine student, athlete, and trumpet player. I aspired to be all those things.

During the summer of about my twelfth year I worked as her gardener. One lovely morning I was weeding her flower bed right below her open kitchen window. I heard this eminent lady talking on the phone with a friend. I listened even more closely when it seemed they were talking about me. Toward the end of the conversation she said quite clearly and authoritatively: "That Bobby Benne would make a good minister."

Bam! I almost fell on my trowel. I couldn't believe my ears! A pastor—that was the last thing I wanted to be. I wanted to be a jock, first an athlete and then a coach. But *she* said that about me, a gangly near-teenager with no real record of accomplishment. What was happening?

For some strange reason I did not interpret her assessment of me as coming solely, or even primarily, from her. It came from God through his Holy Spirit, of that I was sure. She was the messenger of the Holy Spirit who was choosing me to be God's servant as a pastor in the church of his Son, Jesus Christ. The Holy Spirit drove that message into me with such power that I have never doubted its authenticity. I have staked a major dimension of my life—my work—on that conviction.

I did not tell anyone that God had chosen me in a special way for service in the church. Not my friends or parents. Not even my pastor. I was a bit embarrassed that I had been called to "the religion thing" when I desperately desired to be a glorious contestant on the fields of friendly strife. In our town men never talked about religion—though nearly all went to church—but they talked incessantly about sports. I wanted them to be talking about me as an athlete, not as a religious type, which to me and many others had a slight tinge of feminine softness to it.

Internally, however, I began making decisions that said "yes" to God's call. What else could I do when confronted so clearly by his Spirit? So I continued to participate regularly in church activities, especially Sunday School, Luther League (a youth organization), and choir. I tried to follow the Christian moral code, which in the 1950s, unlike today, seemed quite clear. When it came time to choose a college, I decided I had to go to our nearby Lutheran college, Midland, since it provided the prescribed route to becoming a pastor. I turned down several football scholarships to go to Midland, though I never told the recruiters the real reason why.

That powerful call gave me clear sense of purpose in life, a great blessing. From then on it has been "long obedience in the same direction." But even more, that call bestowed on me the deep sense that I mattered to God, that he deigned to give little old me a role in the drama that he was writing for my life and the other lives I would be directed to touch and affect. That "justified" my existence before him. Thanks be to God!

INTRODUCTION

At the conclusion of the divine service of the Lutheran Book of Worship *the pastor enjoins the assembly: "Go in peace. Serve the Lord." To which the congregation responds: "Thanks be to God!"*

I write this memoir out of sheer gratitude for the wonderful life the Lord has given me, but especially for that moment when his Spirit called me to a special role and purpose in life. That's why the main title is "Thanks be to God." I want to reflect on those blessed gifts, whether or not anyone reads about them. It is a great mystery why we were "thrown" into life at a particular time and place and family. No one chooses that, not even our parents, let alone we. But this "thrown-ness" powerfully conditions our lives. Even more of a mystery involves the "who" that did the throwing. H. Richard Niebuhr, one of my heroes, argued that the greatest question of life is: is that which threw us into existence for us or against us? If it is neutral it is against us because it has no support for our aspirations and destiny. But, if we confess and believe that it is *for* us, that makes all the difference in the world. If we believe it is for us, we can say "yes" to it and trust it. Further, we can say "yes" to the particulars of our existence—our time and place in history, the family we have been given, and for the set of callings he has offered us. That holistic "yes" is the religious response inherent in the Christian faith because we believe that the mysterious God who threw us into existence has revealed himself in the Christ event as love. We are enabled to say "yes" with confidence to that which is offered—our lives. The life I have been offered is one overflowing with goodness. Far more than I ever expected or deserved. I want to reflect on that divine bequest, its challenges and opportunities, in this memoir.

But there may be an additional reason or two for this project. First, it may be interesting as an account of the exertions of a practical theologian, one who has engaged Christian ethics with some of the great issues of his life span—the interpretation of the 60s, the debate over the nature and destiny of America, the competing claims of different economic systems, how theology might be relevant for the 21st century, Christian responses to the sexual revolution, and the nature of Christian higher education. I have lived in interesting times, as the Chinese do not actually say, and have encountered and written much in response to the challenges of my own epoch. Perhaps my engagement with them is interesting to more readers than my inner circle of friends. Moreover, while engaging those issues I have come across some of the "great and near great" of each era, not because I was that important but because I had the good fortune to be at the right time and place.

Another reason for writing is to show gratitude for America. Since immigrating to America, both my paternal and maternal families have experienced the opportunities the American Dream has offered. The gradual ascent of each generation of ancestors from lowly beginnings has been inspiring to me. "When I first came to this land, I was not a wealthy man; but I did what I could…and the land was sweet and good." That quote was a frontispiece in one of the books I wrote with a colleague, and it sticks in my mind to this day. America has been good to the Classens and the Bennes, both immigrant families, who in the 19th century left Germany for the daunting adventure of homesteading in the great Midwest.

Finally, my children and grandchildren—and perhaps even my great grandchildren—may find the story of their forebears interesting and edifying. One can live in hope. And I do.

I have organized the book according to the callings Christians have been given: family, church, citizenship, and work. The accounts of those important projects in life have been preceded by the story of one luminous moment I experienced early in life that set me on a purpose that has endured a life-time. The preface has offered an account of that unmistakable call from God through the Spirit to serve him in the church of his son, Jesus Christ. Those interested primarily in my vocation as a practical theologian can leap now to the last chapter—Chapter Four—that depicts that journey. Those interested in the other callings that flesh out my life (and perhaps afford reminders or lessons for their own) may read the chapters on family, church, and citizenship.

I am grateful to the American Lutheran Publicity Bureau, on whose board I have served for many years, for their willingness to publish this book. (How could they refuse?) I am also pleased to have had my friend, Ray Brown, also a member of that board, edit the manuscript. He has smoothed and enlivened my prose in many places.

Grandparents John and Paulina Poledna Benne (1911)

Grandparents George and Mary Punzel Classen (1950s)

Grandpa Classen with horses (1950s)

LeRoy, Herman, Harvey, Ralph, Lawrence, Elmer, Ed, Fred, John, Herman sr.
The Benne 9 with Grandpa John and Great-Grandpa Herman on the far right (1922)

West Point baseball team about 1933
(Dallas at 18 in front row left)

Parents Dal and Irene Benne in 1968
(She is 50 and he is 53)

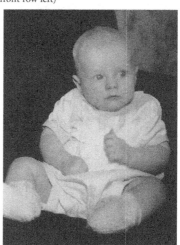
Bobby as a baby

Bobby, Kenny, and Carol in 1946

Bobby as a fifth grade
trumpet player

Bob as a
high school senior

Bob and Joanna Carson on graduation day
in June of 1959

Bob and Joanna on their wedding day,
August 29, 1959

Bob and Joanna with their 4 young children in 1979, from left: Nicholas, Michael, Kristin, Philip

25th anniversary in 1984 with 4 children plus new son-in-law, Christopher Kremer

4 adult children in 2009: Nicholas and Kristin, front row Michael and Philip, back row

Bob and Joanna at their 50th anniversary

Whole family at the beach, 2012

Seven out of eight grandchildren at the beach, 2019; from left: Linnea Kremer, Kai Kremer, Andrew Benne, Alex Benne, Ian Benne, Max Benne, and newest Elizabeth Benne (Dylan Kremer missing)

The whole family of Dal and Irene Benne at her 100th birthday celebration, July, 2018

Bob and Joanna jitterbugging at their 60th wedding anniversary, 2019

CHAPTER ONE
OUR FAMILY—GOD'S GREATEST EARTHLY GIFT

GROWING UP IN WEST POINT: 1937-1955

I was born on May 24, 1937, and baptized on July 24 at Grace Lutheran Church in West Point, Nebraska, by Pastor Klink. My parents were Irene Gertrude Classen Benne and Dallas John Benne. She was 18 at my birth and he was 22. It was the depth of the Depression and neither had a chance to go to college. Both had to get to work right after high school. They met in 1935 in a little restaurant called the Black and White in downtown West Point (pop. 2400) where she was a waitress. They evidently had a rapid courting phase that culminated in their traveling to Omaha (75 miles away) to be married by a justice of the peace on August 11 of 1936. They were too poor to have a church wedding and had to borrow a car to make the trip. In just as rapid fashion as their courting, I came on the scene in a small upstairs apartment on South Lincoln Street, my birth aided by a mid-wife. They soon needed more space and rented a larger apartment on the second floor of a frame house on North Main Street owned by the Kase family. Joe Kase was a harness-maker. My first memory—of anything—was of playing with a new toy tractor on Christmas Eve. Another early memory was being carried on my dad's shoulders to see Wendell Wilkie campaign for President on Main Street in our town in 1940.

My mother was born into a homesteading family from Boyd County in northern Nebraska, the nearest town being Spencer. She was the last of seven children of George Classen and Mary Punzel Classen, who were married in 1900. Grandpa was a kind and soft-spoken man who was part of a larger family that had immigrated to the United States in 1882. Born in 1870, he was twelve when he left the Frisian Islands off the coast of Germany with his older brother, Timmien, his widowed mother, and four younger children. The father had died and they had few prospects on the island. The mother and older brother worked for ten months to earn the $130 the seven needed for passage to America.

After landing in New York they journeyed to Adams County in central Nebraska, a rich farming area. There Timmien rented a farm. At 17 George bought a team of mules and rented a farm for himself. When the government opened Boyd County in northern Nebraska for homesteading in 1890, Timmien and George staked out claims for farms. Both put up sod to build houses, but when they left it unguarded someone stole it. They had to return to Adams County for a year but went back to Boyd County to claim their stakes. This time they guarded their sod and lived in temporary sod houses until they could hire a German carpenter to help both of them build permanent houses.

George was a successful farmer whose hard work and creativity in raising crops, hogs, chickens, ducks, geese, and milking cows led to prosperity by the 1920s. The family possessed state-of-the-art farm equipment and barns. They had a home with running water, indoor plumbing, and electricity, something rare in Boyd County. He refused to give up horses for working the farm; he loved those animals. Though he purchased Ford Model-Ts for the use of the children, he never drove them. All the prosperity came to a screeching halt with the Great Depression and then the Dust Bowl, a particularly nasty combination. The farm reverted back to nineteenth century practices—water pumped by hand from a well, outhouses, and kerosene lamps to light the house.

George and Mary spoke German at home and church; the older children were catechized in German in the country Lutheran church attended by the Classen clan, as well as other German homesteaders. But the children wanted badly to become fully American, so they avoided German and quickly picked up English. My mother, Irene, blotted out her heritage so thoroughly she knew neither German nor where her parents came from in Germany.

Mom, Dad, and I, along with two siblings who came along in 1941 (Carol Ann) and 1945 (Kenneth Gene), would go to the Classen homestead for our summer vacations. We first went to Spencer by a slow train and later by the old used autos Dad could afford. I loved going to the farm because my grandpa would let me ride his horses and go with him on various chores. I also swooned over the home-made bread, butter, and jam my grandmother made. Grandpa was sweet and kind, Grandma tough.

One time she took me with her when she slaughtered chickens. I can still see the poor birds running around spurting blood from their headless necks. I was shocked and refused to eat chicken for a dozen years. Likewise, I was witness to the slaughtering and butchering of hogs and cows. I was a near vegetarian for years following, eating only meat that was safely ground into unrecognizable parts.

Country life was not always compatible with my small town sensibilities. Nevertheless, I enjoyed the contrast between farm life that resembled 19th century pioneer life and our "modern" town life.

Though my mother grew up on that farm, she could not stay long in the midst of the Depression. Upon graduation at sixteen she was sent to help her older sister, Maggie, who had a nasty case of appendicitis. Her sister was married to a farmer whose spread was near West Point, about 160 miles south of Spencer. After she had helped their family for several months, she moved to nearby West Point and found a job as a waitress in that little restaurant where she was asked out on a date by Dal Benne.

Dallas John was the middle child in a family of five—an older sister, Evelyn, and brother, Jack, and two younger sisters, Dorothy and Gladys. His father, John, was the oldest son in a family of fourteen, nine brothers and five sisters. Living and working on a farm north of West Point, the boys organized a "Benne Nine" baseball team that toured northeast Nebraska and challenged town teams in the region. Old clippings say they won pretty consistently. The father of the large brood, Herman Heinrich, was said to have his children baptized in bunches to save on gratuities for the pastor. The family later moved to town into a lovely red brick home that still stands. Sadly, the mother, Meta, died soon after they moved to town.

When they moved from the country to town a mysterious transition took place, one that has never been explained. In the country the family was Missouri Synod Lutheran, but when they moved to town all but one family shifted to Grace Lutheran of the United Lutheran Church in America, the mildly pietist and less ethnic branch of Lutheranism. The latter allowed members to join the Masons, which may have explained the shift.

Herman, the patriarch of the West Point Bennes, was one of two brothers who moved north to Nebraska from the St. Louis area, where the Benne family had first settled. The patriarch of that original set of immigrants, Johan Friederich Benne, had left a little German village named Buer (near Hannover) in 1842 for the New World, specifically St. Charles, Missouri. In Buer Johan and his brothers owned little plots of land but not enough to sustain their large families, so Johan left for America in 1842. Bennes still live in the Hannover area, one member of which told me that the Bennes were originally Huguenots who had been driven out of France in the 16th century. They also assured me that we had no Jewish blood, since everyone had to present their "pure" genealogies to the Nazis in the 1930s![1]

Once in America, most of the Benne family stayed in the St. Charles area—where a number of descendants still live—except for Herman, who came to the West Point area to farm, and his brother, Johan Heinrich, who settled further north in Nebraska.

With such a large set of relatives, my childhood memories are filled with recollections of huge family gatherings at Christmas time and the Fourth of July. Many long tables loaded with all sorts of home-made food. There were smaller gatherings of grandfather John Benne's family spread throughout the year. John had married a woman of Czech (or Bohemian) background named Pauline Poledna. Grandfather John was a gruff, cold, and distant man who was a plumber and windmill builder. After windmills became obsolete, he worked for the town as a handyman. He showed little interest in his grandchildren and not much more in his children. Grandmother was much warmer and interested in us. She, however, had lost all the family's savings in the bank busts of the Depression, and had something of a melancholy aura about her. It was rumored that she had attempted suicide when the family lost all its savings.

My mother did not feel welcomed by the John Benne family, perhaps because my father's three sisters and their families made up kind of an "in-group" of West Point people. Mom was not part of the clan. Whether my mother's perceptions were accurate or not, she felt that way. So our family was somewhat distant from those of my father's siblings, until later when we all grew up. Then my siblings and I tried hard to reconcile with the rest of the family, which effort was successful.

---

1. I was once featured on the front page of *The Lutheran*, our then denominational journal. Somehow a Jewish man saw the magazine in a resort lounge in Colorado. He sent me a note of inquiry: "Are you by some chance Jewish? You and I look like brothers."

My father was the first class into the brand new West Point public school (1st through 12th grades) in 1921, the same school (with the same first and second grade teachers!) my siblings and I attended. Dad was a pretty mediocre student who was held back a year. But he was a fine athlete in all the traditional American sports, but especially baseball. He was a good enough pitcher to be drafted into the St. Louis Cardinal system, where he played for a time in a Nebraska semi-professional league. However, he injured his throwing arm and never played competitively after that. He was only in his mid-20s when he hurt his arm, so I never got to see him pitch. But his love for baseball continued as he coached American Legion baseball and umpired for many years. I, a pitcher like Dad, had the misfortune of being coached by my father. He did not want to show any favoritism toward me, so he compensated by hassling me more than my teammates. This annoyed me enough to exacerbate my tendency to throw hard and wild.

Dad worked in a clothing and shoe store, and then a hardware store, at low wages. Mom stayed at home until all three kids could fend for themselves and then she began baby-sitting around town for some extra income for the family. Our parents were active at Grace Lutheran Church—Mom was in Ladies Aid and Dad in Lutheran Brotherhood. They insisted that we kids attend Sunday School, church, and Luther League. However, we participated in few Christian practices at home; we didn't pray at meals or talk of religious matters. Such reticence was not uncommon among German Lutherans who would die had they been called upon for extemporaneous prayer. Yet it was clear that we all needed to participate regularly in all church activities.

They provided a solid home in which we kids knew they were committed to us in a rock-solid way, though they did not express their affection verbally or physically. That would have been too demonstrative for German Lutherans shaped by the Depression. My mother has fended off hugs as best she can her whole life; at the time of this writing she is one hundred-one and still hug resistant. My father would never had entertained a hug from another male, though in his later years seemed to enjoy those of his daughters-in-law and his granddaughters. Despite their lack of emotional expression, we had a high level of trust in them. Those strong bonds conveyed a sense of support and stability in our family home that was very important in our later lives.

They always "bought the cheapest kind," and were very frugal, but oddly enough would let us kids raid a little box of cash on the top of a kitchen cabinet when we felt we needed money. Though distinctly lower-middle class—we had neither rugs on the floor nor books in our rented apartment—we never felt any real want. Though the cookie jar always seemed empty and the little cartons of ice cream were quickly devoured, we never went hungry or thought we were deprived. We were given freedom to roam the town and come and go as we pleased…as long as we didn't misbehave, which we didn't.

My younger two siblings—Carol and Ken—did well in school and off they went to colleges, Carol to Midland College and then to the University of Nebraska, Ken to Wittenberg College in Ohio, where he excelled in football. Carol started to date her mate-to-be, Floyd Erickson, in high school. In due time, both siblings married—Carol to Floyd in 1963 and Ken to Pat Richmond, whom he met at Wittenberg, in 1968. Children quickly followed: to Carol and Floyd, a boy (Steve) and a girl (Kathryn); and to Ken and Pat, three boys (Chris, David, and Brad). Ken and Pat's three boys all married and had children, nine in all. Floyd and Carol's have not married.

Floyd, an engineer, worked for General Motors and Electronic Data Systems until his retirement. Sadly, Carol died of cancer in 1999. Ken and his wife spent most of their working lives at Wittenberg, Ken in admissions and Pat in education. Ken continues to work for the college in resource development. They have watched over our mother as she has become more dependent with age.

COLLEGE AND GRADUATE SCHOOL: 1955-1965

In our sophomore year (1956-57) at Midland, I met Joanna Carson, who, I was told by a roommate, liked me. That intelligence emboldened me to ask her for a date. When we found we had so much in common—we seemed to be meant for each other—we began dating, "went steady," were "pinned," became engaged on New Year's Eve of 1958, and married in the summer of 1959, right before we embarked in September for a year on a Fulbright Scholarship to Erlangen University in Germany. There we met dear friends, both German and American, whose friendship we have enjoyed for a lifetime. We also traveled a whale of a lot on the least amount of resources imaginable.

Joanna's parents lived in St. Joseph where her dad, Robert, owned a struggling pharmacy. Her mom, Ellen Larson Carson, came from a Swedish settlement in Minnesota and was trained as a laboratory technician. She was definitely the stronger and aspiring of the pair, and kept the family afloat amid the subdued alcoholism of her mate. She cultivated her Swedish background and passed that on to Joanna. Bob died in 1980 and Ellen came to live near us in Salem, Virginia, in 1984. She died in 1994 at 94 years of age.

Back to our Fulbright year in Germany. To our great surprise, Joanna became pregnant during that year and bore our daughter, Kristin, right as we were about to move to Chicago in 1960 for my Ph.D. work at the University of Chicago. Our five years there featured a son—Philip in 1964, as well as an M.A. and Ph.D. in the Ethics and Society Field of the Divinity School of the University of Chicago. Not only was the intellectual life of the time bracing (more about that in a following chapter) but social life among other economically challenged graduate students and their kids was quite enriching. We particularly enjoyed our relationship with Phil and Neva Hefner, who were mentors both academically and domestically to us.

As I was working on my Ph. D. dissertation in 1964-65, the President of the Lutheran School of Theology (Augustana Campus in Rock Island, Illinois) hired me to fill in for a newly called professor of Christian ethics, Franklin Sherman, who was to fill the ethics chair at the new seminary being built in Chicago, but who was yet finishing a term as tutor to Lutheran students at Oxford University. Off to Rock Island we went. There we enjoyed a good deal of camaraderie with the young Augustana College faculty and their families. One of them—an entertaining and irreverent comic by the name of Tom Tredway—later became president of Augustana College. At the seminary I taught with enough gusto that I was invited to fill a new position in church and society—established especially for me—at the new seminary, which was to begin in Chicago in 1967.

CHICAGO YEARS: 1967-1982

So, back to Chicago we went in the summer of 1967. We bought a town house in a co-op development that was built on a whole city block with a central play area for children in the middle of it. It was a wonderful place for our kids to grow up. We added two more sons during our second stint in Chicago—Michael in 1969 and Nicholas, who was a late and unexpected blessing, in 1977. He came as a shock nine years after out third child (Michael) and seventeen after our first (Kristin), but was welcomed heartily. Teaching at the new seminary in the middle of the 60s (I consider 1965-75 to be the 60s; 60-65 was an extension of the 50s) was an exciting experience, as was the intellectual and social life of the large faculty drawn from five ethnic background Lutheran seminaries that merged into the new Lutheran School of Theology at Chicago. Our kids went to the local public schools where they met friends of many ethnic and racial backgrounds.

We had a year's sabbatical in Hamburg in 1971-72 where I wrote my first book and planned another with Phil Hefner. Seven years later we had a second sabbatical in Cambridge, England, in 1978-79 when I wrote another. I wrote more books on two more sabbaticals there in 1985-86 and 1992-93. But equally important as those academic accomplishments was the sustained exposure to life in other countries and cultures for us and our children. Our sabbatical years have been a wonderful blessing of academic life for our family. They demarcate our lives in happily distinct ways. An additional gift was the chance during our Hamburg and Cambridge stays for our three boys to learn, play, and appreciate soccer, which has greatly affected their lives. Philip became a women's soccer coach at Roanoke College and Michael earned All-American honors at Virginia Wesleyan College. Nick played and became a huge fan. They passed their love for the game to their kids so we have enjoyed a myriad of soccer games played by our children and grandchildren. One granddaughter—Linnea—Kristin and Chris' daughter, played and excelled for son Philip at Roanoke College. She later played university soccer in England, where she earned an M.A.

Back to the 60s for a bit more of my parents' lives. My mother in 1965 received a small inheritance from her mother's estate, which my parents used for a down-payment on a loan to buy the local Dairy Queen in West Point. They moved into the rear quarters of the small building and proceeded to work, eat, and live in the DQ. Dad took time to serve on the city council and as mayor for one term. (Political life was not really his cup of tea; he took political disagreements personally.) They also established a teen canteen for teenagers who needed organized social time on the weekends. They were so energetic and frugal at the DQ that they soon paid off the loan and in a decade made enough money—including that from the sale of the DQ—to retire in 1977 and move to Springfield, Ohio, where my brother and his family lived. I was shocked that they had the audacity to move from their comfortable world, which deprived me of a home place in West Point. I worried that they could not make the transition to Ohio. But that transition they indeed accomplished, and lived happily ever after. Truth be told, it was a wonderful move for them.

My brother, Ken, had by this time become Vice President for Admissions at Wittenberg University, while Pat, his wife, taught in its education department. My parents became co-parents to Ken and Pat's sons as well as dedicated Wittenberg Tiger fans. They also had the chance to visit us during four of our sabbatical years abroad, the only experience they had of traveling outside the United States. They and we cherished those visits. (My father had no clue what the currencies were worth in the various countries we lived in and visited, so he would hand me stacks of twenty dollar bills to cover all expenses and more!)

They celebrated their sixtieth wedding anniversary surrounded by thirty-eight of their descendants in the summer of 1996. Dad died a year later on Easter morning, March 30th of 1997, thirty days before his eighty-second birthday. His funeral was on Easter Monday at Grace Lutheran in Springfield, with his committal a day or so later in Mount Hope Cemetery in West Point, next to his parents and brother. Many of his old friends and relatives attended.

My mother continued to live independently in her Springfield home for nearly twenty more years. As she rose through her 90s the family marked those milestones with major celebrations. She broke her shoulder in 2016 and is currently in an assisted living home. The whole family—nearly fifty—celebrated her 100th in July of 2018.

SALEM YEARS: 1982-

In 1982, after fifteen years at the Lutheran School of Theology in Chicago, I was recruited by the then president of Roanoke College, Norman Fintel, to chair its Department of Religion and Philosophy, to occupy its newly endowed Jordan-Trexler chair in religion, and to define and organize a center for which they had already raised a considerable endowment. By that time we were ready as a family to take on new challenges in a different school and location. The school was Roanoke College, of which

I will write more later. As for location, the small town of Salem fit that bill very nicely. It was a family-centered, conservative, Christian, well-governed town of about 25,000 that was fiercely independent from its larger neighbor, Roanoke. There we joined the local College Lutheran Church and met many friends and acquaintances whose connections we have enjoyed for the 37 years we have lived in Salem. However, in the fall of 2016, after 33 years at College Lutheran, we moved our membership to St. John Lutheran in Roanoke, where we are meeting new friends and taking up new responsibilities. (More about my college and church experiences in a later chapter.)

In these Salem years all four of our children married and had their own children, numbering eight in all. The grandchildren's ages run from twenty-nine to three, which reflects the large span of years between our oldest and youngest offspring. They have flourished—though not without some hitches—and we rejoice in their unfolding lives. Kristin (married to Chris Kremer, a legal videographer) has three children—Dylan, Linnea, and Kai—and works as an analyst for the Kroger company in Cincinnati. Philip (married to Stephanie, an elementary school teacher) has three boys—Drew, Alex, and Max—and has coached women's soccer at Roanoke College for 30 years. Michael has sole custody of his son, Ian, and works as a coder for Carilion Hospital in Roanoke. Nicholas, married to Caroline (a Georgetown University Hospital official), has one daughter, Elizabeth, and works at the Government Accountability Office in Washington DC.

The athletic gene which seems to run in the Benne family has been transmitted to the grandchildren: the Kremer's in basketball (Dylan), soccer (Linnea), and football (Kai); the Philip Benne's in soccer; the Michael Benne's in track; and the Nicholas Benne's yet to be determined since Elizabeth is only three. We hope and pray that the Lutheran religious gene in them will be at least as strong as the athletic.

Joanna and I look forward to our sixtieth wedding anniversary in August of 2019. We are both in reasonably good health for which we are grateful, especially since Joanna had a bout with breast cancer in 1987. We have had a long, happy, fruitful, and eventful life together. God is good!

Standing now nearly sixty years after our marriage, I look upon marriage and family life as the most important earthly calling. They not only give us the most intimate experience of unconditional human love in our life on earth, but in doing so they grant us a "foretaste of the feast to come." Moreover, they offer us the wonderful opportunity to cooperate with God in the mysterious and miraculous gift of begetting and caring for new life. And that new life in the long run makes a far greater impact on the world than our efforts in all other callings. Thanks be to God!

Grace Lutheran Church in the 1950s

Bob's Baptismal Certificate

Resurrection window
at Grace Lutheran Church

Good Shepherd altar painting
at Grace Lutheran Church

Star of the East

Confirmation, Palm Sunday,
March 18, 1951

St. Stephen's, South Side, Chicago

Danish custom of dancing around the tree, 1962
(Joanna, Phil Hefner, and Neva Hefner holding Kristin)

Baptism of son, Philip, at Christ the Mediator, Chicago, 1964
(Pr Gerald Kline, sponsors Gerald and Carol Christianson)

Baptism of son, Michael, on right, at Woodlawn Immanuel, Chicago, 1969
(Pr Rick Deines, members of the church)

Kristin as Light-Bearer on Santa Lucia Day, Augustana Lutheran of Hyde Park, Chicago, 1975

Virginia Synod delegation to the first ELCA Church-wide Assembly, 1989 (Bishop Richard Bansemer)

Baptism of grandson, Andrew Benne, at College Lutheran, Salem, 2000
(Pr Dwayne Westermann and Bishop James Mauney)

Marriage of son, Nicholas, at College Lutheran, Salem, 2012
(Pr Wynemah Hinlicky)

St John Lutheran Church, Roanoke, Virginia

Bob with Pr Mark Graham

CHAPTER TWO
INESCAPABLY LUTHERAN

EARLY YEARS: 1937-1955

Grace Lutheran Church in West Point, Nebraska, was built along the Akron Plan—a chancel surrounded by three pew sections. It had a large nave, holding at least three hundred. Above the nave was an impressive dome with a stained glass border. A choir loft—not really a loft but a platform—was situated to the left (facing the chancel) with a large organ between the loft and the chancel. The chancel, of course, had a lectern and a pulpit on either side of the altar. The striking thing about the altar was a painting of Jesus the Shepherd gently carrying a little lamb to safety in the Judean wilderness. I often imagined myself in those arms and still do today.

There were three stunning, large, stained glass windows on each of the other sides of the church—one of the nativity, another of the crucifixion, and another magnificent one portraying the resurrection. A risen Jesus offers peace outside the empty tomb. Under that window sat a row of aged ladies, many of them members of the pioneering families of the town. I had little interest in them when I was growing up though now I wish I would have talked to them. One was a distinguished poet and short story writer whose works are still in print—Amy Bruner Almy.

Above the altar near the ceiling was a circular window with a star—obviously the Bethlehem star—situated above a desert with a palm tree. That window was illuminated in a darkened church at the eleven-o'clock Christmas Eve service as Mrs. Hasebroock (yes, the same one) sang "Star of the East." An enchanting moment forever etched in my mind. When Mrs. Hasebroock could no longer sing that song Pastor Krebs asked me to play it on my trumpet. I stood in the sacristy with the door half-way open and played a muted version of the sacred song. A grumpy old member of the council complained that there should be no such instruments played in the church. In spite of that, I got to perform at several more Christmas Eves.

Unhappily, when the chancel was "modernized" in the 70s, the altarpiece and the window were demoted to a historical display in basement hall in favor of a bland altar with no painting. Several other depredations were executed, including the elimination of the chancel steps that were covered for the Christmas Eve early service when the children performed their "pieces," often to the gentle prompting by the director of the pageant. It was under that covering that a large number of Christmas boxes were stored for distribution to all the children after the program. There was always a piece of fruit and some good chocolates, along with less alluring hard candy.

I was baptized on July 24, 1937, at Grace Lutheran by Pastor Klink, though little was made of that date later on. The sacrament of baptism was not much emphasized in my growing up years, which was a deficit in the piety of the time. Strangely, I have few memories of Pastor Klink even though I was eleven when he left Grace.

My earliest memories at Grace begin with our little preschool group (those born in the late 30s were special because of the low birthrate in those Depression years) being taught in a basement room off the large gathering room. Several of our little band have known each other for a lifetime, something of a rarity. Besides many pipes lacing its ceiling, the little cubby hole had a picture of Jesus confounding the elders. We all sniffled a bit when we were moved to a larger room and deprived of our womb-like security. After that we were taught by women until we "graduated" from Sunday School when we left for college. We were expected to show up every Sunday and did. We were rewarded with perfect attendance pins, the collection of which sometimes reached down to our belts.

I remember little from the grade school years in Sunday School classes but the high school ones were notable. They were taught by Mrs. Blanche Beckenhauer, who posed provocative religious questions to our little class, which stirred up much discussion. She wagered a milkshake that by 1970 humans would be able to control the weather. I took her up on that bet and collected my milkshake many years after our Sunday School time. She was a good sport.

The plenary gathering before we went off to our classes was memorable. Mrs. Guy Thompson offered the announcements and directed the vigorous singing by the room full of kids. She would lead us in scores of rousing gospel songs, whose texts and melodies I remember to this day. At request time we adolescent boys would ask to sing "The Little Brown Church in the Wildwood" so we could sing the bass line—Oh, oh, come, come, come—with our newly changed voices. Mrs. Thompson was quite plump and the fat in her upper arms would jiggle as she directed. She kept good order with a maternal warmth and resolve. Only later did I understand how remarkable this was, considering that she and her husband had lost their only son about that time in an air sortie over the Philippines in World War II.

At about twelve or thirteen we were expected to attend church services upstairs in the nave and sing in the choir if we had any musical aptitude. Mrs. Kotlar, wife of the only atheist in town, its optometrist, led the choir. Mrs. Hasebroock was the star soloist for our weekly anthems. I sat by one of the town's barbers, Carl Bernhardt, who had a deep bass voice and who slept soundly through every sermon. This was not uncommon behavior among the many men who, with their wives and kids, filled the nave. Sometimes I had to nudge Carl when he snored. Carl not only cut my hair but took care of the baseballs at the town team ball games. He sat by a gate close to the catcher and umpire, and would keep them supplied with reasonably useable baseballs. We kids would chase down foul balls that came over the grandstand and return them to him for ten cents.

The Rev. George Krebs, in austere black gown, preached gentle sermons except when he excoriated the Catholics. Nothing could be worse in that era in that locale than a Lutheran "turning" Catholic or vice versa. We didn't know a whole lot of Lutheran doctrine but we knew we weren't Catholics! (The only real rift I had with my parents before college was when I dated a Catholic girl.)

Pastor Krebs also led fairly placid liturgies and prayers from the Common Service Hymnal. Besides not being Catholics, the liturgies and hymns of that hymnal were what made us Lutherans. Otherwise we were pretty much generic Protestants, products of the Americanized Lutherans who came west to missionize the German settlers of our town. Though we were catechized from Luther's Small Catechism and tested over our knowledge of it before the congregation, Pastor Krebs had mercy on us by telling each of us which section of the catechism we would be quizzed on. We were not exceedingly strict doctrinally—in contrast to the Missouri Synod church a couple of blocks from us—but had internalized certain clear moral rules. Those rules—work hard, be frugal, be patriotic, don't complain, have sex only in marriage, don't drink, be honest, be kind to others—were carried as much by the postwar culture as by the church, though the church honored them in many implicit ways. When we confessed our sin at the beginning of our service, we knew what moral rules we had violated.

We had Communion only four or five times a year, with grape juice instead of wine, which were practices our brand of Lutheranism picked up from the generic American Protestantism of the time. The rare communion services were very solemn affairs, though, with the recipients lined up before the chancel and across the church. I was terribly impressed when coaches and teachers from our school would engage so seriously in that sacred rite. This was especially true during Lent, which was the most defined, and somber, season of the church year.

After a year of confirmation training held on Saturday mornings (nothing else offered competition at that time), we were ready to be confirmed before the whole congregation and then ushered to our first communion. Besides my earlier sense of call, I can recall few times in my life when the presence of the Spirit was so intense. Receiving the bread and wine (grape juice) for the first time conveyed a sort of ecstatic presence of Christ that is still palpable.

In high school we participated in Luther League, a national youth organization of the United Lutheran Church in America whose local chapters were generally led by a young adult member of the church. Neva White, who later married my friend, Phil Hefner, was our leader. At the League's Sunday evening meetings we were a bit more immersed in the teachings of the faith, but mainly enjoyed social life with other teenagers from our congregation. Luther League also provided us with occasions to interact with other kids whom we met at regional and national gatherings. A goodly number of them we met later at our Lutheran college, Midland. Luther League was an effective instrument of the church for incubating young leadership, especially pastors. It was also pretty good at getting boys to meet girls of similar religious convictions.

The local churches at that time provided much of the social life of our town. Grace Lutheran itself had several men's softball teams that played in leagues sponsored by the many Lutheran churches in the county. Of course the Lutheran men never played the Catholic men, who had their own ample leagues. During the winter it was bowling leagues. The men also were active in Lutheran Brotherhood, which performed many service and charitable deeds. Pictures of their chapters showed hundreds of men, young and old. My dad was once president of Brotherhood. The women had auxiliaries of various sorts, many of them devoted to the support of foreign missions and the church's charitable institutions. Foreign and domestic missionaries often visited the church, which connected us in a direct way to their efforts. The women also provided the teaching corps of the church, and took care of all the logistics of church coffees, suppers, and other social events, which were many. The church even provided a New Year's Eve alternative to the dancing and carousing of the secular celebrations. The dignified men and women of the church played ridiculous roles in games of charades. From the mid-40s on the church was full of returning veterans and their wives... and the many babies that had been postponed by the war. The other churches in town, St. Paul's (Lutheran Church–Missouri Synod) and St. Mary's, experienced similar expansions. Certainly this seemed like Christian America—to be an American was to be a Lutheran or Catholic, and vice-versa. And I do mean either Lutheran or Catholic. Our town had virtually nothing in between except a tiny Congregational Church that couldn't sustain a Sunday School and an Evangelical United Brethren Church whose pastor almost died of starvation before the church itself expired. But the Catholic and Lutheran churches in town and in the county flourished.

In spite of the blandness of Grace Lutheran's occasionally milquetoast Protestantism, my years there were formative for me. After my call to the ministry, I participated faithfully in all the facets of the life of the church. All in all, Grace provided a solid foundation for my young and naïve faith. I seemed to be ready for the next chapter, going off to college.

RELIGIOUS LIFE AT MIDLAND COLLEGE: 1955-1959

Midland College, our Lutheran college only thirty-two miles away in Fremont, was the natural step for me since I was committed to preparing for the ordained ministry. Young people of the church were challenged to consider Midland by its peppy admissions director, Ralph Ritzen. I did not need to be recruited since my trajectory was already set. Though I was honored by coaches personally visiting me from the Universities of Nebraska and Wyoming—and letters coming from other schools—to recruit me to the football programs of their respective schools, I was adamant in my path. Besides, Mark Haight, the football coach at Midland had already offered me a scholarship to play at Midland. So now I could have my cake and eat it too. I could academically prepare for seminary while I played football and other sports at college.

I had very idealistic notions of Midland as a Christian college. I was shockingly disabused of those expectations at our first fall football practice, before the other students at Midland had arrived on campus. I was sitting amid a large group of players gathered on the ground outside the locker room, waiting for the first football practice to begin. Around the corner of a dorm came a guy with his duffel bag on his shoulder. "Cripes"—although that is not the expletive he really used—said a tough-looking, big, Korean War veteran, "here comes one of those damned namby-pamby pre-theological students. If we get many like him we are bound to be losers this season!" Yikes! Coupled with the vulgarity and profanity expressed by other similar types of guys, I reconsidered whether this was the kind of Christian school I had expected. When the upperclassmen began asking what majors we freshmen would be electing, I sheepishly replied: "psychology." I briefly went back "into the closet."

But that wasn't for long. When the bulk of the students arrived and the faculty began interacting with us, I felt more comfortable admitting I was a "pre-the." Indeed, there were many of us young men headed in that direction, some even to become missionaries. Not only that, the student body as a whole was solidly Lutheran, though few trumpeted their religious identities. We didn't have to since at least ninety-percent of the student body was Lutheran, along with a similar percentage of the faculty. The Lutheran Student Association was enormous, rivaled only by the German Club, which drew many male students to its Christmas party where girls were obliged to offer a kiss when asked to toast the season.

We had required chapel five times a week. Pity the poor chaplain, Dr. Strickler. Chapel was not recognizably Lutheran. It featured a hymn, short homily, prayer, and another hymn. Sometimes the college choir would sing. Often outside speakers and preachers were brought in. By and large, the student body was obedient to this onerous requirement, but there were instances of pranks and gentle protests—mainly sleeping—by a recalcitrant minority.[2] By and large chapel did not provide a profound religious experience.

Surprisingly, but strongly conditioned to do so, most of the student body went to church on Sundays even after being force-fed during the week. The four or five large Lutheran churches in Fremont were the preferred destinations. It was exciting to explore churches that were different from our home churches, and sometimes even to visit churches of other denominations, especially if those students, like I, had never been in other Protestant churches. A Presbyterian church in an upscale part of Fremont had a learned preacher who drew us to repeated visits. But the flashy preacher in the new Congregational church pulled a stunt I have never forgotten. At the climax of his sermon on the grace of God he suddenly held up his gold Bulova wristwatch and said: "Would

---

2. I was a member of a secret society, advised by a daring sociology professor, whose purpose was to stimulate school spirit preceding football games by pulling pranks of various sorts. One had to do with hiding a banner saying "Beat Wesleyan" on a wall behind the lectern in the chapel. We planned it for the day when the academic dean, William F. Zimmerman, was speaking at chapel. An alarm clock sounded and the banner unfurled behind him as he spoke. Dignified and unperturbed, the Dean didn't miss a beat. He noticed the banner out of the corner of his eye and proceeded. The chapel was full of scarcely hidden smiles and giggles.

anyone in the congregation like this watch?" Everyone was a bit nervous and embarrassed so he had to make the offer several times. Finally, some brave soul said he would take it. The preacher walked over to him and gave him the watch. "That is what the grace of God is like; we only have to receive it." he said. Perhaps no one ever forgot the illustration. That pastor had a son, Larry Becker, who, after having overcome a serious case of polio, entered Midland and often sat next to me (Becker-Benne). He later got his Ph. D. in philosophy at the University of Chicago and taught for many years at Hollins College in Virginia. He and his wife produced a magnificent encyclopedia of ethics.

Young Lutheran men found plenty of young Lutheran women of serious religious conviction, and vice-versa. I met Joanna Carson, my wife to be, in our sophomore year. I was looking for a good-looking but unspoiled girl of strong Christian belief who gave off signals that she liked me. She was looking for a serious Lutheran—perhaps one headed for the ordained ministry—who was bright, athletic, and sober! Her father was an alcoholic and she wanted no further bouts with an addictive personality. I passed that test and we proceeded through the various phases of courtship: dating, going steady, pinned, engaged, and then marriage soon after graduation. In each phase we lived up to the Christian sexual ethic we were taught by the church and culture of the time. It was not difficult to find Christian young people who believed and acted similarly.

Though not many of the faculty actually engaged their faith with their teaching, they were all supportive of young Christians developing into adult Christians. Several did in fact demonstrate faith-learning engagement. Sarah Hawkinson, the drama teacher who also taught Shakespeare, would point out the Christian anthropological assumptions in Shakespeare's character depictions. Gilbert Lueninghoener ("Loonie" to us), professor of geology and astronomy, demonstrated how Christians could believe in geological—and biological—evolution and still be Christians. When he would take us to our little planetarium on campus, he would have us all lean back in our reclining chairs while he projected the starry heavens on the ceiling. "Ah, the glory of God," he would elate.

We were required to take four courses in Christianity: Old and New Testament when we were freshmen, and Christian Doctrine and Christian Ethics when we were seniors. The freshmen courses were very pedestrian, taught by pastors who had had little education in biblical theology or criticism. It was a shame that we were not more challenged by a deeper approach to biblical study. But the senior courses were different. The courses were taught by a newly arrived Ph.D. out of Hartford, Allan Hauck. We read the spanking new *Handbook of Christian Theology*, edited by Dean Peerman and Martin Marty. It was an exciting compilation of theological essays of the neo-orthodox movement. I was stimulated by it, but the real life-changing book came the next term in Christian Ethics. We read *An Interpretation of Christian Ethics* by Reinhold Niebuhr and I was blown away. I will reflect upon that more in the chapter on my calling as a Christian teacher and writer. It was a genuine intellectual awakening. I also took two independent studies—one on logic and one on Kierkegaard—from our new professor.

These studies honed my ethical sensibilities to the point that I refused to pray with the football team when the new coach gathered us in a huddle to pray for victory. I also refused to go to chapel the day the chaplain honored the two students—boy and girl—who in campus-wide voting were found to exemplify high Christian ideals. I won the vote, but thought it unseemly to have a contest and gain a reward for something so "external." Who really knows the inner workings of an individual? I was Lutheran enough to know that my inner state might be worse than many other colleagues. At graduation I gave a rather preachy valedictory address entitled "Success or Less." It was a Kierkegaardian critique of what I thought was the materialism and conformity of the 50s. In retrospect, I suspect the audience thought correctly that I was a bit self-righteous and presumptuous. But I was young and idealistic, and more than a little naive.

Another source of intellectual stimulation were the lively bull sessions we had late at night in Men's Memorial Hall. Midland, though small and rather undistinguished, had the fortune of being the westernmost college of the United Lutheran Church in America. The ULCA had churches scattered all over the Midwest, Northwest, Southwest, West Coast, and even Hawaii. Pastors from those widely scattered churches had often gone to Midland and advised their young people to attend there. Loyal Lutheran young people often followed their pastors' encouragement, so Midland was gifted with many bright young Lutherans from all over the western part of the country. My inner circle of friends became academics, physicians, pastors, and teachers. It was a remarkable gathering of young men and women who later fared well.

After studying until about 10 PM, a half-dozen of us would take turns running out for pizza or doughnuts and then eat and talk. The conversation ranged from politics to girls, but mostly focused on religious and philosophical questions. It was so lively I would not be able to sleep, so I often felt tired during the day, especially since I played two or three sports each year. Those intellectual exchanges were generally better than most class discussions and they forged friendships that have lasted a lifetime.

RELIGIOUS LIFE IN GERMANY: 1959-1960

After marrying Joanna on August 29th of 1959, we took off for a Fulbright year at the University of Erlangen in Germany. Though we didn't get much out of the staid state German Lutheran churches, we were exposed to something completely out of our comfort zone. The American Lutherans who were studying at Erlangen included pastors enthusiastic for the liturgical movement that was just getting going in America. We low church

Lutherans had never experienced anything like the high-church services that the American pastors—along with some German cohorts—celebrated. Liturgical garb and shades of the Oxford Movement. Smells and bells all the way! The culmination of the year was a "high mass" at the Lorenz Kirche in Nuernburg. At least a dozen pastors were in the liturgical procession; Joanna and I were the only congregants. After kneeling on the hard stone slabs for the first half-hour of the service, we retreated to our chairs and watched the great display for the next hour or so. It was an unforgettable learning experience.

RELIGIOUS LIFE IN GRADUATE SCHOOL: 1960-1965

Graduate school continued the pattern of us young people enjoying the benefits of church life without taking responsibility for them. Right in the University of Chicago neighborhood was its famed Rockefeller Chapel. It had a fine organ and organist, as well as a paid professional choir. The pastors were dignified liberal Protestants who crafted fine sermons that focused mainly on social ethics. Congregants filled about half the large nave, which was also used for commencement exercises. The music was inspiring, but the worship was not.

The Chapel hosted a memorable event in the early 60s when Karl Barth visited Chicago on his first and only trip to the USA. The nave was jammed; we sat in a balcony and peered down as Barth lectured on a "Theology of Freedom," which kind of buttered up the audience. The political freedom that America pioneered and preserved was analogous to the freedom of the Gospel. But more memorable was his little dual with Jaroslav Pelikan, then a professor of church history at the University of Chicago, who lacked little in the realm of self-confidence. In the panel discussion after his lecture, Barth cited a line from a Mozart opera, first in Italian and then in English. Pelikan, who also revered Mozart, countered with a longer passage in Italian.

Barth, not to be bested, responded with an even longer section. This continued until it was clear even to the combatants that it was a crowing contest between two roosters, not edifying instruction for the audience.

The weekly chapel at the Divinity School was thoroughly liberal Protestant. Speakers tried to avoid any text that was beyond the bounds of reason alone. So we quickly migrated to Lutheran churches on the South Side, of which there were many. My mentor, Phil Hefner, had connections to a Danish background church, St. Stephens, at 85th and South Maryland, so we followed him and his family to worship there. It was a parish of the "Happy Dane" American Evangelical Lutheran Church, which was head-quartered (with Grandview College and Seminary) in Des Moines. The church followed the Danish Lutheran tradition shaped by N.F.S. Grundvig, whose famous motto was: "First a Man, then a Christian." The tradition carried a kind of Lutheran humanism that celebrated folk life—music, food, dancing, crafts, story-telling. It had a number of folk schools scattered in the Midwest. It had a wonderful hymnal containing fine liturgies and hymns. Its celebrations of Christian holidays in the homes of its parishioners were phenomenal.

When we first came upon it in 1960 it was nearly 100 percent Danish. We were invited to many homes—what food and drink!—but especially to the home of Ben Vennergrund and his wife, Ella, who provided us with many a Sunday dinner of Danish delicacies. (Ben, a Swede, had the good fortune of marrying a Happy Dane.) The pastor, Harry Andersen, was also gracious. Harry was a pacifist who suffered badly as a conscientious objector in World War II. He was both humble and brave. He later became a bishop in the Evangelical Lutheran Church in America.

As it happened, the neighborhood was changing. One Sunday morning a black couple showed up at the front door of the church and they were advised by the ushers that they would be more comfortable in a black church down the street. Harry hit the ceiling and called a church council meeting at which it had a hard decision to make. Would the council and church follow the pastor, who passionately believed in a church that welcomed black people, who deserved to hear the gospel at St. Stephen's, and who would no doubt be the future of the parish? Most of the older, fearful Danes were on the other side. They wanted to maintain the ethnic cohesion of the parish. The debate was close. Ben, who was the president of the council, held deeply racist views that had been recently confirmed by the sexual assault on his daughter by a black man in the midst of the chaos that accompanied neighborhood change. But Ben also knew that he was obligated to do the right Christian thing. He absented himself from the meeting, vomited in the alley, and returned to cast the deciding vote to accept black folks as members.

Our five years of graduate school in Chicago offered other interesting opportunities. Since we had been introduced to "evangelical catholic" Lutheranism in our year in Germany, we attended two "liturgical" Lutheran churches, one a Missouri Synod student congregation at the University of Chicago named St. Gregory of Nyssa. It was very small but had been adorned by Jaroslav Pelikan and his family. The other was a Lutheran Church in America mission called Christ the Mediator on the near south side of Chicago. It had a mixture of black neighborhood folks and white professionals from the nearby Michael Reese hospital. We had our first son, Philip, baptized at the latter.[3] Both churches offered weekly Eucharist, something of an unusual practice in those days.

---

3. One of our friends who had visited Israel gave us a little bottle of water from the Jordan River, from which we mixed a few drops into the baptismal water of our daughter, Kristin, in 1960. Four years later we used drops from the same vial for the baptism of Philip. However, mid-way through the service I realized with horror that by now the water was most likely contaminated. So right after the baptism I took baby Philip to the first bathroom I could find to wash off the contaminated residue of the baptismal waters off his head. After that the vial was tossed and further baptisms of Benne children were done without the benefit of Jordan water.

RELIGIOUS LIFE AT THE LUTHERAN SCHOOL OF THEOLOGY AT CHICAGO: 1965-1982

I began my teaching vocation in 1965 at the Rock Island, Illinois, campus of the soon-to-be formed Lutheran School of Theology at Chicago. That school had been Augustana Seminary, the seminary of the Augustana Synod, which was the Swedish background Lutheran church in America. At the time the seminary was nearly all male. (The only two women attending the seminary were being taught to become parish educators.) The daily chapel services featured fine singing by the young men and excellent preaching by the faculty and senior students. Family church life was at First Lutheran Church in downtown Moline, Illinois. I had already developed a strong commitment to urban ministry in my graduate school days so we joined a large, stately, but gradually fading, downtown church. The church building was magnificent in a classically Swedish way, but the religious life was unexceptional.

In 1967 we moved back to Chicago where I became the seminary's first assistant professor of Church and Society. Since I was committed to the great idealistic movements of the early 60s—civil rights, urban renewal, and community organization—we sought an inner city church, which wasn't all that difficult because the new seminary was built right adjacent to the University of Chicago on the South Side. The South Side was replete with many ethnic-background Lutheran churches that were struggling to survive amidst the neighborhood change that was sweeping the South and West Sides of Chicago.

One of those churches was Woodlawn Immanuel, located in the impoverished Woodlawn neighborhood right south of the University of Chicago. It had been a flourishing church with a large nave, ornate altar, and even a gym. As providence would have it, one of my prize students from the recent Rock Island campus days—whom I had inspired to enter urban ministry—was the new pastor. He and his family lived in a parsonage right next to the church in a very tough neighborhood. Almost all the whites had left the church and the neighborhood, but the pastor, Rick Deines, had inherited and recruited a group of strong black women who made up the core of the church. We had only a few men, who were difficult to bring into a female-dominated church. Rick and his wife, Dixie, devoted great energy to the renewal of Woodlawn Immanuel and its neighborhood.

He was fueled and shaped in his pastoral leadership by his immersion in the Ecumenical Institute, a community of highly charged existentialist Methodists from Texas. They had taken over the nearly defunct Ecumenical Institute that had remained in Evanston, Illinois, after having been organized following the World Council of Churches meeting in 1954. The leaders of the E.I. moved it over to a seminary campus on the West Side that had been abandoned by a denomination fearful that it could not lure students to such a dangerous location. They transformed it into a kind of Protestant monastic community dedicated to the renewal of the church and of the neighborhoods in which the churches lived. The Institute had developed highly disciplined intense courses in the Christian faith, anti-racism, and neighborhood transformation. The courses were part pedagogically brilliant and part brain-washing. It was difficult to discern where one started and the other left off. The theological course was called Religious Studies I and worked though the key Christian doctrines—God, Christ, Holy Spirit, and Church. The courses were shot through with the Christian existentialism of the day. Woodlawn Immanuel became a hotbed of training for those courses.

The anti-racism course was designed to make all participants admit that they were racists and needed to listen to black people for their marching orders to overcome racism. We pressed that course on a number of pliable white churches, but were abruptly halted in our tracks when a group of highly educated Jewish women from Hyde Park (the University of Chicago neighborhood) refused to admit they were racists. We had to revamp the course.

Part of the EI approach was to keep the structure and texts of the classic liturgy for worship, but to replace the staid music with catchy popular melodies. So Sunday morning services featured existentialist sermons on the Word and lively liturgies that all could sing. The worship at Woodlawn Immanuel became quite infectious to seminary students, and many came to supplement the rather small gathering of regular members. Evangelism was difficult in the neighborhood, though, because of a large number of popular black Baptist churches.

Moreover, the leadership of Immanuel spent far too much time with unrealistic schemes to transform the neighborhood. After a time, mission aid from the national church (Lutheran Church in America) was cut off because of our failure to grow and become independent financially. Without that financial support, Pastor Deines and his family had to leave. Phil Hefner (who was ordained) and I tried to lead the church for some months after Pastor Deines' departure but finally had to throw in the towel. We concocted a moving service for closing the church that became a feature article in the church's national magazine, *The Lutheran*, in 1973.

It was a long and grueling span from 1967, when we joined Woodlawn Immanuel, to its closing in 1973. I would not want to go through that again. At times, however, participating in its worship, its teaching, and its missional attempts was exhilarating and Spirit-filled. Our second son, Michael, was baptized at Woodlawn Immanuel in 1969. We learned much about the travail of black people and their communities and the enlivening possibilities of the Gospel for all concerned in such circumstances. It was indeed an enriching experience for us.

In all this the Ecumenical Institute's approach was a mixed blessing. The basic Religious Studies I was helpful in the theological formation of the laity, but had to be "Lutheranized" if it were to be useful to Lutheran churches. Its intensity and lingo tended to produce "in-groups" and "out-groups" in the life of churches. Its "social transformation" courses tended to sow real tensions and break-ups in congregations. The latter course became destructive enough that the LCA forbad its pastors to participate in or teach them. Since I was an "insider," I was asked by the church to write a critique of the EI, and I did. It languishes in total obscurity in the church's archives. I later adapted the Religious Studies I course for use in the seminary's training and outreach programs. In fact, I still use some of its concepts and diagrams in a course I do on theological interpretation of film. They are contained in a book I wrote in 1993 entitled: *Seeing is Believing—Visions of Life Through Film*.

Religious life at the seminary was shaped by daily chapel at which, to the consternation of the faculty, only a portion of the student body attended. The liturgies were done very well, there was weekly Eucharist, and the preaching by the chaplain and the faculty was excellent. As we navigated the 60s there were some attempts to politicize seminary worship, but cooler heads prevailed. It was only in later years at the seminary—after I had left—that feminists agitated for major language changes in the worship of the seminary and church.

After the closing of Woodlawn Immanuel we moved our membership to the newly built Augustana Lutheran Church of Hyde Park, right across the street from the seminary. Its architecture was striking and the parish was a mixture of leftovers from its days as a Swedish background church—hence its name, Augustana—and seminary families, as well as local Hyde Parkers. A social activist pastor had just departed when we became members and had left the congregation in pretty bad shape as far as membership and finances go. Our newly called pastor was of the "evangelical catholic" tradition—he later became an Episcopalian and was re-ordained!—and focused his ministry on liturgy and sacraments.

The parish was dominated by academics from the seminary and the University of Chicago. It had a superiority complex. Its music was excellent, performed by musicians and singers who were, for the most part, unbelievers who were committed to a high aesthetic. Gospel hymns and nineteenth century British hymns were treated with contempt, if sung at all. Preaching was as weak as its liturgy was strong. Sadly, it had a non-existent youth ministry program and weak confirmation training, right at the time when our older two children were in need of such nurturing.

The church hosted a Pregnancy Testing Office sponsored by a local private organization. The church council, of which I was a member, was told that after the testing was done, pregnant women were given information about birthing the child as well as facilities to get an abortion. *Roe vs. Wade* was promulgated in 1973 so abortion services were widespread. However, when my wife became unexpectedly pregnant in 1977 and used services of the office, she was handed a list of abortion facilities—nothing else—when she tested positively! The women in the office were stunned when she said that she had no intention of aborting. That meant the church was hosting an organization promoting abortion. To the credit of the council, it terminated our agreement with the office after I protested strongly.

ROANOKE COLLEGE AND SALEM, VIRGINIA: 1982-

Shortly after I arrived at Roanoke College in 1982 it gave up its sparsely attended Sunday service for weekday services. Since the college protected no special time for chapel, its Lutheran chaplains have always had to compete with many other organizations for attendance. It's always been a losing battle, though the chaplains have offered a solid weekday service for the small number of students, faculty, and staff who attend. I attended for many years but recently have found the experience discouraging enough to slack off.

For thirty-three years our family membership was at nearby College Lutheran Church, with its historic connection to Roanoke College. Those years, too, were a very mixed bag. The first pastor was a glib fast-talker, who served ineffectively and dishonestly, and departed in disgrace as he left his devoted spouse for the wife of a college professor. He did not think it a disgrace because he shamelessly finagled a call to a new parish in a nearby small town, against the wishes of the Virginia Synod bishop. He made both transitions without losing a Sunday. Needless to say, youth ministry and confirmation, as well as his preaching and leading worship, left much to be desired. The congregation rapidly lost members.

A renewal of sorts took place when the church was able to call one of the former assistants to the Virginia Synod bishop. When the new the Evangelical Lutheran Church in America (ELCA) was formed in 1988, a new bishop was elected who brought in his own assistants. Those of the former bishop looked for new calls. College Lutheran was fortunate in acquiring Pastor Dwayne Westermann, who presided over a lively new phase in that historic church's life. College Church was founded by the first president of Roanoke College and had been served by many distinguished pastors. It had a grand building made of sandstone from a nearby quarry. A lovely high altar graces a large nave. Westermann's call to College Church brought an exciting new interval in which many alienated members returned and new people joined.

Westermann preached finely crafted sermons in a mellifluous voice. They were brief and to the point, often with fine imaginative anecdotes. Sometimes the theology behind his sermons was a bit dubious, but not very often. He gently pushed the church in an "evangelical catholic" direction by introducing more elaborate vestments—such as the chasuble—and by moving toward weekly Eucharist. Indeed, it seemed that College Lutheran was the "high-church" choice in the Roanoke valley. The congregation burgeoned for a time. Those who had fled the earlier pastor came back. Three or four adult Sunday School class choices were available. The lower grades of Sunday School were well attended and staffed. A young organist and director of music, Aaron Garber—came on board. He was also a composer who pioneered a choral society for the whole metropolitan area. Worship and music flourished. Two of our sons were confirmed, one son married, and three grandsons baptized later at the church. We gained many friends.

I taught regularly throughout the time at College Lutheran and served on its council for several terms. I also served on the Virginia Synod Council and lectured in many of its churches. I befriended bishops Moyer, Bansemer, and Mauney as the years passed by. Joanna participated in a ministry to the elderly at the local Lutheran senior facility. We witnessed the transition of both Virginia Synod charities (social services, senior facilities) from church supported, "Lutheran institutions" (Lutheran-led with many Lutheran volunteers and patients with programs embedded with discernible Christian substance) to secular institutions. Both charities grew like topsy but at the cost of their soul. Yet they serve their clients well.

Youth ministry was still undeveloped so College Lutheran decided to call a second pastor who would be responsible for youth ministry and evangelism. The church was poised to grow ... but it didn't. An economic downturn complicated a situation in which the new pastor was not as enthusiastic and vigorous about his assigned role as the church and Westermann had hoped. We hit a financial crisis in which we had trouble paying our bills. Membership declined and in-fighting emerged. Fortunately, our situation was eased when the associate pastor received another call.

Though his departure meant an easing of the financial crisis, a good deal of damage had been done. Westermann turned more of his attention to his African mission work, which was quite admirable. He took a goodly number of the congregants on mission trips to Tanzania. He got the church to support Tanzanian students. He preached regularly about that venture, sometimes giving the impression that the "real Christians" were in Africa, implying that we listeners left something to be desired.

He directed less energy into pastoral ministry; he became more distant from the inner workings of the church.[4] Finally, after some years of diminishing interest and energy, he resigned.

The church had a long interval without a pastor; more people left. Finally, we (I was on the search committee) found two promising candidates. The first turned us down but the second—actually a married pair of pastors—said "yes." William Wiecher and Wynemah Hinlicky (along with three children) came on board. They had had successful ministries in separate congregations in upstate New York. The search committee hoped that Bill could reach the young men and boys who seemed less and less attracted to the church, and that Wynemah could attract the younger women into service to the church. We hoped that their *bona fide* shared ministry would lead to the renewal and growth of the congregation.

Sadly, it didn't work out. After a few exciting months of a joint ministry, Bill was deployed as an Air Force Reserve Chaplain. He had no sooner returned than he was called up again. This happened repeatedly until we began to realize that all this was not mandatory but that Bill actually preferred that armed forces chaplaincy over parish ministry. This meant that Wynemah had to carry on the College Lutheran ministry by herself as well as raise three growing children. Both pastors were strongly committed to the evangelical catholic version of Lutheranism and Wynemah slowly elevated the liturgy to a "higher" level, e.g., throwing away the plastic cup shot glasses and organizing a more elaborate liturgical ritual for the distribution of the Eucharist. She also strongly encouraged the Eucharist at funerals. To some congregants, though, she came off as haughty and authoritarian.

---

4. Pastoral care of the sick and shut-ins slowly diminished to the point that some congregants came to believe that the pastor visited parishioners only on their deathbed. When a ninety-some pillar of church was hospitalized but had every hope of recovery, he allegedly was so shocked at the appearance of the pastor (was this the end?) that he was reluctant to see him.

As the ELCA gradually moved toward accepting gay marriage and partnered gays as pastors, at which it succeeded in 2009, she became increasingly uncomfortable, orthodox as she was. She publicly mentioned her admiration for and participation in events held by the Coalition for Reform (Lutheran CORE), an organization that resisted the drift of the ELCA. I was a member of that group and encouraged her and Bill to attend its gatherings. (I will write much more about my participation in the "resistance" in the chapter on work.)

A key member of the Virginia Synod/ELCA loyalist group within the parish reacted strongly to her mild dissent from the trajectory of the ELCA and verbally attacked her ferociously in a meeting of the mutual ministry committee. Though she was supported by others who were also worried about the direction of the ELCA, she was "pacified." She never brought up "hot button" issues again, nor did she attend any more gatherings of CORE.

Though she performed her ministry of Word and Sacrament faithfully, and was especially effective in pastoral care, her confidence was diminished by that intimidation and the congregation limped along. She resigned in the spring of 2017 to join her husband, who was continuing his chaplaincy in the Air Force Reserve, and to care for her ill mother. After her departure many congregants inaccurately blamed her for the struggles the church was experiencing.

While the church had many traditionalist Lutherans who strongly disagreed with the trajectory of the ELCA, "belonging trumped believing" for the vast majority. Moreover, the bishop of the Virginia Synod was a member of the congregation. Before 2009 he had mildly resisted the drift of the ELCA, but when the revisionists won, he conceded quickly. There was little desire or effort on the part of the congregants to leave the ELCA, so I never tried to lead an organized effort for College Lutheran to depart. It would have futile and we would have lost many friends. Everyone in the congregation knew where Joanna and I stood because I was never quiet about what we proposed or opposed. Indeed, I was not shy to teach orthodox Christianity in the courses I taught.

College Church has recently called a young new pastor who is generally orthodox and a rising star in the Synod. The parish, like many others, believes that they can survive and live "the apostolic faith" in a larger church (both regional and national) that has lost a good deal of it. We wish the pastor and the parish well because we have two sons and their families in the parish. We hope the pastor can kindle a robust faith in them, overcoming their rather casual participation in the church.

From the formation of the ELCA in 1988 I had a queasy feeling that the church would move in the liberal Protestant direction by conforming to the progressive agenda, especially with regard to sexuality issues and the nature of evangelism. While the local parish, College Lutheran, kept on an orthodox path, it was painful for us to remain in a congregation of the ELCA. We have an ecclesiology that is holistic—the church is a corporate body that includes the international, national, regional, and local. One cannot belong and possess loyalty to only one expression or geographic locus of the church.

Across town in the Cave Spring area of Roanoke County is a large Lutheran church named St. John. It has been pastored from 1987 on by a highly effective orthodox pastor, Mark Graham, who is committed to evangelism. He knows how to grow churches and does so with great success, enlarging the physical complex and bringing in new people, most of whom were not cradle Lutherans During the early part of his ministry he was more in the American "evangelical" spectrum than he was in the "evangelical catholic" construal of Lutheranism. Mark has a high view of biblical authority and is resolutely orthodox.

In 2004 he was joined in the St. John ministry by a dynamic and gifted academic, Gerald McDermott, who was then teaching at Roanoke College. Gerry had slowly morphed over the years from the Baptist tradition to the Anglican. Mark and

Gerry were a very lively and creative pair and the church grew. And it grew also in its clarity about its identity and mission. Somewhat influenced by McDermott, St. John became a "liturgical, sacramental, orthodox, and missional Lutheran church," or what I would call an "evangelical catholic Lutheran church."

When the ELCA finally departed from Christian teaching on sexuality issues in its assembly of 2009, Mark and Gerry immediately prepared to lead St. John out. In a series of votes the congregation decided by more than a 70 per cent affirmative margin to proceed to more orthodox pastures. Sadly, but not surprisingly, about 20 per cent of the congregation that wanted to remain in the ELCA left St. John angrily. Belonging to the ELCA and its Virginia Synod trumped believing for them. Schism was a greater offense than heresy. It was a difficult time but the pastors and congregation now knew they had an orthodox congregation. It was a powerful winnowing process. Since there was no North American Lutheran Church at the time, St. John became a member of Lutheran Churches in Mission for Christ, a loose association of churches, congregational in polity.

In 2015 St. John voted to join the North American Lutheran Church several years after its founding. I was an active participant in the various resistance movements against the ELCA's false teachings and spoke to many congregations about the crisis in the church. Soon after the NALC founding, I was elected to its Commission on Theology and Doctrine. I have great admiration for the Bishop and staff of the new church. So, for Joanna and me it was a "no brainer" to leave College Church for St. John. We had to align our local church membership with a national church that had fought the good fight to maintain faithfulness to authentic Lutheran teachings and practices. We were received into membership at St. John on Reformation Sunday of 2015. Though we had invited a number of our friends from College Lutheran to witness our reception into St. John, none came. Indeed, no one has followed us from College Church to St. John, which is either a commentary on our leadership capacities or on the power of "belonging over believing." Perhaps both.

We left College Lutheran as amicably as possible in the spring of 2015 and have not looked back. I had known Mark Graham for many years; I was a reader for his D.Min. thesis. I had taught and visited there many times over the years. Becoming members there felt like going home. St. John has many orthodox lay people who want the straight Law and Gospel message. It is a magnet also for evangelicals of other denominations who are looking for something more churchly. It is genuinely active in mission projects and is graced with half a dozen young men preparing for the ordained ministry. Without an organized stewardship approach it still ends the year with surpluses, which it gives away. It has a talented young church music director, as well as a newly ordained, competent-far-beyond-his-years, associate pastor, Myles Hixson. I am honored as a Christian teacher when several dozen people sign up for the courses I offer. Joanna and I feel completely at home.

In the Trinitarian formula that introduces my evening prayers, I conclude by invoking the Third Person thusly: "In the name of the Holy Spirit, who has brought me to Christ through the church and who gives purpose to my life." From the cradle to the present day, the Lutheran church has enfolded me into the Body of Christ in a marvelous way. Before I could even know what was going on, I was baptized into a mystical union with Christ at Grace Lutheran Church in West Point, Nebraska. I was nurtured in Word and Sacrament by loving pastors and teachers, and experienced the warmth of hundreds of older adults and younger friends. When I visit my hometown in Nebraska, I always head for Mt. Hope Cemetery where many of those saints are buried. Many names on the headstones bring memories of that warmth and love. My father—my 101 year-old mother is still living in Ohio—my grandparents, and great-grandparents, as well as many, many relatives and friends rest there as silent witnesses to the faith, our faith.

I am grateful to God for the church life we had later in Fremont (Midland College years), in Chicago (graduate school years), in Woodlawn and Hyde Park (Lutheran School of Theology at Chicago years), and finally in Salem, Virginia, where we belonged for thirty-three years to College Lutheran and now for four years to St. John. We are particularly delighted to have our local and national churches in synch. Together they provide a centrist orthodox Lutheranism that edifies us greatly.

Over this span of years there were, of course, ups and downs, but we rejoice that we have stayed in the tradition that the Lord placed us. The Lutheran tradition carries profound insights into sin and grace that continue to edify and sustain us. Its teaching on vocation is so illuminating I have organized this book around it. Lutheran worship has a dignity and depth that provides the proper context for Word and Sacrament. Lutheran hymnody in its vast array of ethnic sources is wonderful. (Joanna and I have had to pare down our selection of hymns to fifteen to be sung at our funerals! Of course that is too many but it indicates how many we love.) The Lutheran friends that have abounded in our journey have been precious to us.

From 1965 onward we were able to take up our churchly responsibilities in response to Word and Sacrament, so now we not only receive but contribute. Listing all the offices and roles we have played in these various Lutheran churches over these many years would be tedious for the reader. It has been a long journey—over eighty years—but a blessed one. We wouldn't have it any other way. And, as it seems, neither would our Lord. Thanks be to God!

West Point, Nebraska, in the 1950s

West Point Public School K-12 (until 1976)

Lovely Elkhorn River Valley

Coach Cox exhorting his Cadets, 1954

Legion baseball team, Dad on left, Bob in center, 1955

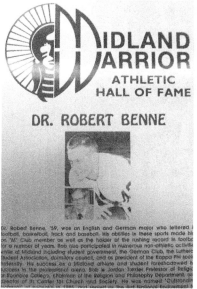

Athletic Hall of Fame plaque,
Midland College (University)

Quarterback at
Midland College, 1958

Bob losing his last race to his grandson, Max (2010)

Festive table of Fulbrighters, MS Berlin, 1959

University of Erlangen basketball team,
Bob front and left, 1959-60

Soviet May Day Parade in Berlin, 1960

Ban the Bomb March led by Bertram Russell (London, 1960)

High Mass at St. Lorenz in Nuernberg, 1960
(Celebrant John Damm, Assistant to left Ted Jungkuntz)

Farewell party at Martin Luther Bund, Erlangen, 1960
(from left: Lois Jungkuntz, Bill Weiblen, Ilah Weiblen,
Ted Jungkuntz, John Damm, Joanna, Cora Foster, Bob Foster)

Martin Luther King, Jr., at Soldier Field in Chicago, 1963

Playing tennis at the Quadrangle Club, University of Chicago (1967-1982)

St Edmund College Dining Hall, University of Cambridge, 1992

View from backyard in Salem, Virginia (summer, circa 1990)

View from backyard in Salem, Virginia (winter, circa 1990)

CHAPTER THREE
LIVING THE AMERICAN DREAM

1937-1955

Like being born into my family, and into the Lutheran church, being an American was not a choice. I could possibly have chosen to take different routes later in life, but at the beginning I was ineluctably a Benne, a Lutheran, and an American of the Nebraska sort. I have sketched my narrative as a member of the Benne family and the Lutheran Church, which immersions I not only accept but I embrace with gratitude and joy.

It is the same with being an American. When pondering the title for my memoirs I originally thought a nifty title would be: "Beyond All (Low) Expectations—the Memoirs of a Practical Theologian." But I finally rejected that because it centered too much on what America has offered me rather than what God has given me, which is far more extensive. Nevertheless, that discarded title conveys the great appreciation and loyalty I have for my country, which, in the final analysis is also a gift of God.

Now, don't get me wrong. I do not believe that America can do no wrong: as a great power it is inevitable that such power has been used wrongly at times. Nor do I believe that the United States is a Christian nation in the sense that it is strongly guided by a clear and coherent Christian culture. America was closer to that kind of guidance system in my youth, but even that era certainly had its faults. Women's roles were strongly constrained while blacks and Native Americans were highly disadvantaged by racism, though we were aware of neither. Along with great gains in recent decades we are now also faced with a fractured culture with significant elements hostile to the Judeo-Christian tradition. But let's not get ahead of the story.

Family, church, and America were all intertwined in my formation, but I have tried to distinguish each strand for the purposes of this memoir. Growing up in a small Nebraska town in the 40s and 50s is where I will begin. West Point, Nebraska, is in northeast Nebraska, 30 miles north of Fremont and 75 miles northwest of Omaha. It lies in the Elkhorn Valley and is surrounded by agricultural counties with small towns dotting the landscape. The land is fecund and much of its corn is fed to cattle gathered into large feedlots. Cuming County is named the Beef County because it feeds more beef for market than any other county in the USA. West Point, about 2500 souls in the 40s and 50s, is the county seat.

Northeast Nebraska is a checkerboard of European ethnic groups who settled in distinct communities for support and camaraderie. West Point's population was heavily of German background, which meant that the Lutheran and Catholic churches were large, with only one or two other denominations minimally represented. But right east of us was Oakland, heavily Swedish, west of us were farms and towns peopled by "Bohemians." Germans predominated in most of northeastern Nebraska with scatterings of Scandinavian and Eastern Europeans. There were a few Anglo-Saxon names. Besides those of European heritage, there was a tribal reservation 30 miles to the north of West Point, but we rarely saw its inhabitants except when we played their high school, Macy, in athletic competitions. The closest

African-Americans lived seventy-five miles away in Omaha. The only African-Americans I saw in those formative years worked on a paving gang that came to town from Omaha. Those poor fellows were the objects of much curiosity.

Given the dominance of the European heritage, it is not surprising that there were still strong vestiges of European languages and customs during my growing up years.

A couple of memorable experiences of those vestiges: late during World War II West Point hosted a rather large contingent of German prisoners of war. The young German POWs were housed in the big barns built for the annual county fair. They would go out each morning in trucks to work on the farms in place of the American men who were deployed in the armed forces. There were no escapes attempted; the young Germans were glad to be in West Point rather than on the Eastern Front. After work they would play soccer in the open fields behind the barns. They hit the ball with their heads! I'd never seen such a sport. In the evening they would gather outside their quarters with the old Germans from town, though they were separated by a big fence. The young Germans would sing sentimental Volkslieders, joined by the townsfolk who still knew German even after the Great War had rendered silent much of the German-speaking. Both groups would tear up, the young Germans from homesickness and the old West Pointers from nostalgia for old times. I was so moved that I began retrieving some of the German culture my parents had abandoned. I played my trumpet in a German band sponsored by a country Lutheran church. I learned a little German from the old timers. During the war I learned to draw all the American and German war planes, and would sketch gigantic air battles—dog fights—between the combatants. All this stimulated my desire to learn more about my German heritage.

While West Point was and is dominated by agriculture, I was actually a town boy. My dad trained to be a shoe-maker and shoe repairman, but later became a salesman in a men's clothing store and then a hardware store. We lived in rented houses and then in an apartment situated above two taverns. We were definitely petit-bourgeois—lower middle class. We had linoleum floors, no central heating, few books in the house, and not enough bedrooms. For all my years at home I had to share a bedroom with my brother while my sister shared one with my parents for her early years. During my pre-teen years my mother rented a room out to Catholic girls who would board with us while they went to the Catholic high school in town. My mother always had salmon loaf on Fridays to cater to them. The house had only one toilet in the basement and one bathtub upstairs. We kids bathed in wash tubs in the basement on Saturdays. The adults shared the sole bathtub upstairs. It was a pretty cramped arrangement.

When I reached high school we moved to an apartment above two taverns in downtown West Point. Everything important—stores, school, church, park, playground—was close by so we walked everywhere, as did most of the townspeople. My dad bought old used cars during my pre-teen years but purchased a relatively new '49 maroon Studebaker when I got half-way through high school. I thought it was really nifty and loved to drive it through my later high school and early college years. It had an "overdrive" that achieved the astronomical miles-per-gallon efficiency of about 27 miles. I rigged up the sound system with rear speakers but never could get the engine to sound like a V8.

The growing up years were golden. As little kids we roamed about town and gathered in the park and on playgrounds for pick-up games of baseball in the summer and football in the fall. Sleigh-riding down the steep snow-packed streets in the winter. In the summer evenings the neighborhood kids would play hide and seek: Ollie ollie-oxen free! Dogs and cats roamed with us. No one heard of crime or danger. Our house was on a highway in those early years. My dad brewed homemade beer in the basement. We would sit on a swing on the front porch and watch the traffic go by while we passed a pan full of home brew (nicely iced) down the line. I was permitted to drink with

Dad and Mom but my younger siblings weren't. But we were warned not to drink away from home where it was illegal for the under-aged. And I never did until I was 21.

From about twelve years of age Dad got me summer jobs. I was a water-boy for the crews who built the new hospital. I pushed wheel-barrows of cement for the new swimming pool. I hoed cockleburs. I did garden work. I de-tasseled corn. I worked at the new pool. I helped construct the new telephone exchange. I washed down and tuck-pointed the old school's brick façade with an Omaha crew. In my college years I managed the town pool, which meant teaching many kids to swim and a lot of life-guarding in the sun without a cap.

Besides the church, the other main institution in town was the school. The public school was K-12 (although we did not have kindergarten when our class entered school because of World War II), as was the Catholic school, which was about equal in size to the public. The Missouri Synod Lutherans had a K-8 primary school, which then fed into the public high school, as did the many country schools that had K-8 schooling. The country schools were numerous and small, often taught by young women right out of high school who had nothing more than "normal training."

The public school was a large, handsome brick building that was the pride of the town when it was built in 1921. I love that building. Dad entered school the first year it was open. He had the same first and second grade teachers as I and my siblings had, Miss Kase (first grade) and Miss Bernhardt (second). Because of the low birth-rate in the late 30s, our classes were small. We did coloring books in Miss Kase's class and had rest periods when we lay on towels on the floor. One of the poor boys in our class, Leonard, who had lost his mother, often went to sleep and would be allowed to sleep on for a while by Miss Kase. Later on, our third grade teacher noticed that Leonard could not see well so purchased cheap glasses for him at Hesteds, the local five and dime. We were drilled in phonics in Miss Bernhardt's second grade class. She kept a little chart on the front of her desk that kept track of how many books we read from the school and town libraries. Each book was symbolized by a gold star. The first inkling that I might be academically oriented was when the stars indicated that I read more books than my classmates. My mother says I talked before I got teeth at one year of age and memorized the texts of the books she read to me so that I could recite them back to her, acting as if I could read. She must have read a lot to me and helped me learn to read at a young age. I was a regular customer at the town library. Miss Frahm, the librarian, steered me to the books of A.P. Terhune and Jack London. I peered through the stereopticons at National Geographic slides. Hoping I wouldn't get caught, I even sneaked furtive glimpses at pictures of naked African women. Further, I secretly looked up a few informative entries on sex in *Encyclopedia Britannica*.

Pretty much the same small group of kids with whom I went to Sunday School accompanied me through the grade school years. We had spinster teachers except for the sixth grade when we had gorgeous Miss Magary, whom all the boys adored, but who was quickly taken away by marriage. We learned basic grammar, math, and writing (the Palmer Method, first in pencil and then in fountain pen) in grade school and junior high. Once our seventh grade teacher, Miss Furchert, probed our class as to what we had in mind for our life's work. Mischievously, and since I was operating my own little shoe shine stand, I offered that I wanted to be a shoe shine boy. "Bobby Benne, "she exclaimed, "you do not want to be a boot-black!"

We had much fun after school playing pick-up games or going to each other's homes, where stay-at-home moms offered us snacks. In the junior high years we began to play organized sports after school, basically supplying "scrubs" for the varsity teams. Football in the fall, basketball in the winter, track in the spring. In the summers we began our baseball with the Midgets in late grade school, then the American Junior Legion in high school. The baseball teams brought the Catholic and Lutheran boys together on the same teams. The swimming pool played the same function for social fun after summer work or baseball. It was especially nice for Lutheran boys to mingle with Catholic girls and vice versa.

Though the high school was small, it offered not only the standard classes but also three sports for the boys (the girls had Girls Athletic Association games), band, smaller instrumental ensembles, choral music, journalism, declamation, Future Farmers of America, Future Homemakers of America, junior and senior plays. Everyone was expected to participate in at least a couple of extra-curricular activities. I participated in all three sports, band (as well as solo trumpet, trumpet trio, brass sextet, dance band), choral music (mixed chorus, madrigal, quartet), journalism, and the junior and senior plays. Social life was ample, with many school dances featuring the high school dance band, the Acorns, led by our dynamic music teacher, Ed Hanna. I played trumpet with the Acorns so I didn't get to dance much.

The most important contribution of the high school to the town, however, was to offer high school sports contests. The townspeople showed up for the games and cheered on—or heckled—the young athletes. It was an honor to be a good musician in the band or an excellent student, but far better to be a fine athlete. My freshman year in high school featured a senior class of really fine athletes who excelled at the state level. Many went on to play college and armed services sports. They were coached by Al Bahe, whom I revered. That made it doubly painful when, as a ball carrier for the junior varsity, I hesitated at a wide-open hole and Coach Bahe pulled me out for a slow and nonathletic classmate. I never again hesitated to run to daylight.

My sophomore and junior years were a mixed bag; excellent music under Ed Hanna but two years of declining athletics under a new coach who did not understand young men. But then came Duane Cox as our new coach my senior year. Duane was a master of adolescent psychology. He provided one of the most powerful moments of "common grace" in my life. I had been deflated by the prior coach who only knew how to chew me out, which I didn't need. I needed a word of affirmation. Here is how it came: the Thursday before our first game Coach Cox had all the guys sit around him on our practice field and he went down the list of starters…and gave reasons why he picked them. He left me until the end and then said: "and my quarterback for the year will be Benne. What's more, since he is a lot smarter than I am, he will call all the plays on the field." Wow. Was I elevated and elated. I called plays the whole year and led us to a winning season….and made All-state quarterback. I also got to play with and against two future Nebraska Cornhusker and then professional football players: Robert Jones and Pat Fischer, both Huskers and then Washington Redskins. I also did well in basketball (All Conference) and track (my long-jump record of 22' 2" held for 35 years).

Coach Cox's "word of grace" gave me confidence not only in sports, but socially. Up until that senior year I was awkward around girls. But I was elected King of Homecoming and the cutest girl in the senior class was Queen. After a hesitant kiss during Homecoming ceremonies I then began dating her. Finally, it didn't work out but the year was fun. After that I had enough confidence to ask other girls out, including a Catholic girl, much to the consternation of my parents.

The summers before and after my senior year were particularly delightful. Laboring at odd jobs for a bit of money, working out in preparation for fall football with some of my older heroes, dating girls, showing off my diving skills for the Catholic girls at the new swimming pool, playing baseball for my dad's team (I struck out 18 in one game against Norfolk), hanging out with friends, cruising Main in friends' cool new cars, listening to Italian-flavored popular music right before rock and roll, adoring our new coach and his family, playing in band concerts on warm summer evenings in the park, and enjoying the county fair…what more could a young guy ask for?

I was valedictorian of the class in 1955, along with other honors. It was a small pond. But what a wonderful start in life.

Participation in instrumental and choral music, journalism, drama, sports, as well as excellent instruction in several subjects (especially English and science). I learned enough in those areas to appreciate them the rest of my life. A coterie of good friends, some quite bright. The West Point education made for holistically developed young people. What's more, everyone had an equal chance to develop. It didn't matter whether you were the child of a doctor or of a farmer, or as I was, the son of a shoe-repairman. There was genuine equal opportunity to enjoy the American Dream's promise to rise as high as you can.

What made these formative years particularly golden was that the culture—the meanings and values that guided the larger society—was coherent and clear. America was great and good, right and wrong were clearly etched, the world was trustworthy, and even popular music was shared by all generations. The coherent culture may have led to a "conformist" culture and politics; there didn't seem to be much difference between Republicans and Democrats. Ike, who'd grown up in a similar social setting, was revered by all. So we young folks didn't pay much attention to politics.

1955-1959

While no one in our immediate family had gone to college, it was natural for me to do so. I wanted to get an education in preparation for adult life as well as take the next step toward the ordained ministry. My accomplishments in high school led to an open door to go to Midland College, 32 miles down Highway 275 in Fremont, a "big town" of 20,000. The college was filled with young people similar to myself, the first generation to go to college. Only a few students had parents who had college degrees.

Paying for college was easy in those days. What I made in my summer jobs, combined with a modest scholarship to play football, paid my tuition, fees, and board and room. My parents gave me a small allowance to get by each week. Few, if any, left college with debts. Students chose their majors and worked their way through an ample liberal arts core. The faculty were supportive, competent ... a few were inspiring. The main teacher for my English major, Herman Gimmestad, loved the literatures of Iceland and the Great Plains. Both genres caught my imagination and I read widely and vowed to meet an Icelander when I got to graduate school. I had a romantic longing for peoples and cultures in remote and difficult climates. The sagas of Iceland and the immigrant literature of the Middle West captivated me. I also did a German major to capture my ethnic heritage and learn another language.

I also got to play and letter in four sports—four years of football, two of basketball, and two of track and baseball. I was versatile enough to get elected to Midland's Athletic Hall of Fame. But my real claim to fame in football, my main sport, was to quarterback for four years against the Hastings College quarterback, Tom Osborne, who became a draft-pick of the 49ers before he became the legendary coach of the University of Nebraska Huskers.[5] My other claim to fame was in Midland College baseball, where I pitched against Bob Gibson when he pitched for Creighton University before he became a St. Louis Cardinal Hall of Famer. He was wild, fast, and mean, with a well-deserved reputation for knock-down pitches. The Midland Warrior players were glad to take three quick swings and sit down safely. Needless to say, we lost to those greats in both football and baseball.

I met my first black persons at Midland. Both played football so I knew and befriended them. They seemed lonely and isolated so I made it a point to have conversations with them,

---

5. For those who follow football, the fifties saw the T-Formation fully take over from the Single Wing. And there was the belly option play: the quarterback running along the line—ball hidden on hip--with option of handing off to a slashing fullback or halfback, or keeping the ball for a sprint around the end. This style of play grew out of the plains states, and was as revolutionary as the more recent West Coast Offense or 4-6 Defense. Truth be told, I didn't hand off much.

mainly about music and sports. I had a memorable debate with Morris Meadows about the relative merits of classical versus jazz music. I also met my first gays. One was very effeminate and had a tough time among other guys, especially football players. He was beaten by a football player who thought he was "coming on" to him. A close friend and I, appalled by such treatment, took the gay guy to a doctor. The poor fellow, though a fine piano player, left Midland soon thereafter. Gay life in those years was not very gay.

Over the four years I rose to the top of my class and gave the valedictory address upon graduation. But more important than that was winning two major fellowships: a Woodrow Wilson and a Fulbright. What excitement to interview for those prestigious awards and then be awarded! When I got the news of the Fulbright scholarship I ran across campus and immediately told Joanna. We planned to marry right before we left in September for a Fulbright year at Erlangen University in Germany.

I also excitedly told my Greek teacher, a young German who taught at the local Lutheran seminary, of my good news. He gravely told me that I was not prepared to study at a German university and that I should decline it. A bit chastened but by no means convinced that I should turn down a Fulbright, I wrote my friend and mentor, Phil Hefner, about the professor's dour assessment. "Nonsense," he said, "the US government isn't sending you there for a graduate degree; it's sending you to be a good ambassador of the USA and to absorb another culture." That happily reinforced my inclination to go for it.

I postponed the Woodrow Wilson for a year in favor of doing the Fulbright. Upon return I had planned to go to a Lutheran seminary, probably to Central Lutheran Seminary in Fremont, but the Woodrow Wilson had to be used at a "secular" graduate school, not a seminary. Again, my mentor Hefner, who was already at the University of Chicago Divinity School, persuaded me to go there after my Fulbright year.

The college years were pretty apolitical. I read the Fremont and Omaha papers in the lobby of the men's dorm, but the sports pages were of more interest to me than the front page. I was aware of the nuclear stand-off and of the McCarthy fracas, but they seemed remote. "Doctor Strangelove" never really bothered us. The Korean War was over and the many veterans we had at Midland talked little of their years in the military. Most were married and lived off campus.

Midland College was another link in the American Dream. Like many Lutheran—and other denominational—colleges, it was an instrument to civilize, Christianize, and educate a new generation for responsible life in church and society. It succeeded.

THE FULBRIGHT YEAR: 1959-1960

Right after Joanna and I married in late August we flew to New York (our first flight and first trip to that city) and boarded the MS *Berlin* with 200 other Fulbright students to Germany. Among the students were a number of recent graduates from Concordia Lutheran Seminary in St. Louis. We immediately befriended them and still treasure those friendships. But before we went to Erlangen where I was to study Reformation history, we participated in the Experiment in International Living in Tuebingen, where we were hosted by a Latvian family, the Lucases, who had fled to West Germany at the close of World War II before the Soviets took over their homeland. The husband and father of the family had returned to the West only two years earlier after twelve years in a Soviet prisoner-of-war labor camp. He was a broken man, reduced to taking care of rabbits at the university's experimental lab after having been a teacher in Latvia. The wife had fled with four children from Latvia, burying one along the way. But she was strong and resolved to make a new life in Germany. We had never been around people who had suffered so greatly and it was a deep learning experience to hear their story and see how they struggled to survive and then succeed. (One of their sons later became mayor of Tuebingen.)

When we reached Erlangen we looked up a German family, the Horns, whose daughter had dated an acquaintance of mine, Jack Faudel, whom I knew from baseball days in West Point. Before we left he gave us the name of the family and encouraged us to meet them, which we did. As it happened, their 19 year old daughter, Gisela, had just decided to accept Jack's invitation to emigrate to America and in time become his bride. She was the Horn family's only child and when she left we filled the vacuum she left in the family's life. What a providential opportunity—to become intimate members of a German family, Walter and Else Horn, in our year abroad. Walter also had spent time in a Soviet camp but was not as damaged as the poor Latvian fellow, though the mother's nerves were badly damaged by the stress of WWII.

The Horns introduced us to other German families of a generation older than we, and we enjoyed real immersion in German life for a year. Besides the academic life, which I will write more about later, we got to travel and socialize with other American students. We traveled nearly everywhere in Western Europe on the lowest budgets ever. The Americans in Erlangen gathered for every American holiday. A number of us fellows—along with several Hungarians who had just escaped Hungary after the upheaval in 1956—played basketball for Erlangen University before Germans knew how to play basketball. We became stars (legends in our own minds) and were only defeated when we faced another German university fielding more Americans than we.

We were able to travel very extensively because Joanna earned travel money being nanny for an American colonel's family, the Perrys, at the American base in Erlangen. Though inexperienced, she did a great job caring for their four kids and a large, American-style home. The colonel himself was embarrassingly anti-German and we had to keep our mouths shut during his many tirades. When he took me shopping in the town to translate for him—he knew not a word of German—I re-translated some of his boorish comments to make them less offensive to merchants and officials.

One remarkable experience occurred when the Fulbright Commission flew all us students at German universities to a conference in Berlin in late April of 1960. There we heard Willy Brandt and other German dignitaries. We visited important sites in and around Berlin and ended our stay by watching the May Day Parade in the Soviet eastern section of the city. What an experience! At that time Berlin was still an open city so citizens could move back and forth between zones. So over to the east we went to view rows of decorated Russian officers, tanks, canons, artillery, and foot-soldiers in parade down Unter den Linden. We had never seen an adversarial power up front and center. Unbeknownst to us, Gary Powers in his U-2 had been shot down over the Soviet Union by an anti-aircraft missile that very day. Quite an international incident followed but we were all back at our universities when the news actually broke.

Though I did not do serious academic work during the year, my mentor's advice about the purposes of being a Fulbright student held true. We were there to immerse ourselves deeply in another culture and travel widely. In doing so I quenched my desire to know more about my German heritage, and we also acquired a thirst for international travel and living. Twelve years later we were to come back to Germany for our first sabbatical in 1971-72. We were also to be good ambassadors of our country, which I believe we were. We got to know many Germans and comported ourselves with respect for our host country, West Germany. What an opportunity for a lower-middle class boy from a small town in Nebraska! The American Dream fulfilled yet again. Happily so, for in the next years it was to be sharply tested by the onslaught of the 60s.

GRADUATE SCHOOL IN THE PERIOD OF LIBERAL IDEALISM: 1960-1965

As noted elsewhere, I believe the authentic 60s didn't get started until 1965 and lasted until 1975. Thus, my graduate school years were experienced during what I call the period of "liberal idealism" (1960-65). I used my Woodrow Wilson Fellowship to go to the University of Chicago Divinity School, mainly because my friend and mentor, Phil Hefner, was there and "sold" it to me. I admired him very much and his words meant a lot. He more or less said: "come on board. It's a great place to study." And indeed it was. It had developed "dialogical fields" that immediately gained my attention. One such field was called "Ethics and Society" and that beckoned me with great persuasive power. I had read some of Reinhold Niebuhr's works in college and had been inspired by the theological ethicist, Walter Kuenneth, at Erlangen. Though Reformation history was also attractive, the field of Ethics and Society became irresistible when I realized that Chicago was right in the midst of three great social movements—civil rights, anti-poverty, and community organization.

The early 60s was a time of great optimism and idealism in America. John F. Kennedy was elected in 1960 and lent an exuberant, youthful, and even glamorous aura to the "New Frontier" times. He gave the whole country confidence that the great problems of America could be overcome in short order. Martin Luther King's civil rights movement had been going on in the South but soon came to the Second City. The anti-poverty movement gained momentum, stimulated by Michael Harrington's *The Other America*, and the community organization movement led by Saul Alinsky-inspired organizations was developing right next to the University of Chicago in Woodlawn.

The most influential professor I had in Ethics and Society was Al Pitcher, who was involved deeply in all three movements and reported on them vividly in our classes with him. He was stirring; we were stirred. The American Dream that most of us students had experienced in our own lives—and in that of our parents'—had the chance to be extended to the black and the poor. And the church could be an effective participant in that heady opportunity. Indeed, for us the church was viewed mainly as an instrument of social transformation.

We students participated directly in these movements and indirectly though the teaching of Al Pitcher and others. By the time I got out of the Divinity School in 1965 I was ready to burst with the desire to inspire younger students with my "liberal idealism" and with a fresh idea of what the church was all about. I will write more about my intellectual development during these graduate school years in the next chapter.

TEACHING IN ROCK ISLAND IN THE OLD AUGUSTANA SEMINARY: 1965-1967

After I had passed my doctoral exams in the fall of 1964 I worked on my dissertation the rest of the year. One day I was summoned by Dean Jerald Brauer to his office in Swift Hall of the Divinity School. He told me that he had recommended me for a visiting professor of ethics position to Karl Mattson, President of the Rock Island campus of the new Lutheran School of Theology at Chicago. That campus had been named the Augustana Seminary, the only seminary of the Augustana Synod, the Swedish-American Lutheran church. It was to join a new seminary next to the University of Chicago in two years, ceding its lovely campus on a hill to Augustana College. Karl Mattson's brother, "A.D." Mattson, had just retired after many years of teaching Christian ethics and his position needed to be filled for two years until the new seminary began, at which time Franklin Sherman, then teaching at Mansfield College in Oxford, would take the position in Christian ethics. Frank was a decade older than I and had been a student of George Forell, the influential Lutheran ethicist of the Lutheran Church in America, which had just been formed by a merger of a number of ethnic Lutheran churches. Sherman was also a University of Chicago Divinity School Ph.D., of whom great things were expected.

I eagerly met with Karl Mattson at a lunch and naturally accepted the temporary position he offered me. (One of my friends at the Divinity School was Gerald Christianson, who had studied at Augustana Seminary. He told me that Mattson was proud of his student days under Reinhold Niebuhr and it would be a good strategy to talk positively of Niebuhr, but note that Niebuhr had a weak doctrine of the Spirit. Jerry had remembered that Mattson made that criticism of Niebuhr. So I followed his advice. Mattson was obviously delighted with my perceptive critique and smiled warmly as he offered me the position.) . I didn't even have to write a resume.

I was so excited by my "liberal idealism" that I hit the seminary like a storm. The sem had been pretty insulated from the excitement of the early 60s and I was ready to inspire it about the church as a transforming agent in society, especially among the poor and black people of the inner city. I taught vividly about the civil rights, community organization, and anti-poverty movements that I had been a part of. By the end of the year I had convinced the majority of the senior men (all the ministerial students were men at that time) to commit themselves to ministry in the inner city. That was, of course, a bit foolish because many of them were not really prepared or fit for such ministries. However, a number of them were, one of whom, Rick Deines, became our pastor when we returned to Chicago in 1967. He pastored Woodlawn Immanuel, a declining Lutheran church in a poor black community right south of the University of Chicago, It was a foregone conclusion that we would join that parish.

This depiction of my life in America in this period of "liberal idealism" is an important chapter in my American journey. From a fairly naïve view of America gleaned from my Nebraska youth, I had now had come upon a serious critique of America in my studies and in my experience on the South Side of Chicago. But what was surprising—at least from the point of view of the 21st century—was the confident enthusiasm that the problems facing America could be overcome. After all, with John F. Kennedy in the White House and a new generation in charge, we were on the "New Frontier." JFK said: "Ask not what your country can do for you; rather, ask what you can do for your country."

Seemingly, all things were possible if we answered that challenge with all our hearts and our minds.

TEACHING AT THE LUTHERAN SCHOOL OF THEOLOGY: 1967-1982

My teaching at Augustana was apparently strong enough to convince the administrators of the nascent seminary in Chicago to create a new position for me, Assistant Professor of Church and Society, in addition to the position in Christian Ethics that was then filled by Franklin Sherman. The new Lutheran School of Theology was intentionally founded in 1967 next to a great University—the University of Chicago—in the midst of a large city. This idealistic move by the Lutheran Church in America was done at the height of mainline Protestant membership, prestige, and affluence. The President of the Lutheran Church in America, Franklin Clark Fry, appeared on the cover of *Time* magazine. LSTC was there to prepare ministers for service in locations that ran the gamut from impoverished urban neighborhoods to Midwest farming communities. The excitement of such a venture was contagious; students poured in from the whole network of Lutheran colleges as well as other colleges and universities. Nearly one hundred young men—and a few young women—showed up for each entering class. Most of the faculty members from four merging Lutheran seminaries came to Chicago to teach in this exciting venture.

Little did we expect what lurked around the corner, though signs were already there in the 1965 riots in American cities and the escalation of the Viet Nam war, which elicited anti-war organizations and activism. Liberal idealism was about to end, and with its collapse came a challenge to me in three of my callings—my life as an American, my work as a professor, and my calling in the church. Things would never be the same after I struggled with and then came to terms with the cataclysmic 60s and their fallout in the 70s and early 80s.

The three callings are so intertwined that I will place my detailed reflections on intellectual matters in the following chapter. Suffice it now to offer a brief outline of the happenings.

I began teaching at LSTC from a liberal idealist perspective—that America had a good chance to overcome its problems by positive action by government, community organizations, and the church. Such teaching inspired only for a short while. Liberal idealism was soon outflanked by a far more critical—even revolutionary—interpretation of the challenges before America. The civil rights movement became Black Power; the student anti-war movement became an anti-American movement fueled by revolutionary expectations; the beginnings of radical feminism, gay rights, and environmental alarm made their appearance. An apocalyptic hue enveloped the country, especially in its urban university centers such as the University of Chicago, the nearby neighbor of the new LSTC.

"Power to the people" rallies erupted in the neighborhood. Martin Luther King was assassinated in April of 1968, toward the end of the first academic year of the new seminary. Robert Kennedy was assassinated in the late summer. The turbulent Democratic Party Convention was held in August of 1968. Anti-war speeches, rallies, and marches popped up all over the country, but especially in Washington. Radicals demanded an end to capitalism and the ushering in of socialism. The Weathermen—a revolutionary group of former University of Chicago students—performed violent attacks around the city and country, often aimed at police, who were termed "pigs."

A remarkable set of happenings occurred during the 1968 Democratic Convention. Richard John Neuhaus, then a Missouri Synod pastor in Brooklyn, was elected Democratic delegate of his district to the convention. Neuhaus, like the rest of us young professors at LSTC, was as an activist on the Left. After the day's convention agenda, he would come down to the South Side late in the evening and regale us with tales of his political activities, as well as his participation in marches, demonstrations, and arrests. The living room at Hefner's home was full of young Lutheran activists, smoking pipes and drinking bourbon, though Neuhaus actually preferred scotch. At a moment of high drama, Neuhaus prophesied that "a small group of brave men could alter the course of history at this hinge-of-history moment." There was little doubt who belonged to that elite group. In a stunning reversal, however, Neuhaus, chagrined by the Roe vs. Wade decision, soon left the Left because he could not convince it to embrace the pro-life cause. He also never questioned the genuineness and good intent of American institutions and would insist that protests begin with the singing of "God Bless America." In time he migrated to neo-conservatism and made a distinctive mark on American public life with his writings and his journals, premier among them *First Things*.

Students at the new seminary caught the radical fever. They protested frequently and finally brought the seminary to a halt, demanding a new curriculum. Hard to satisfy because a goodly portion of the seminary students were avoiding the draft, the activists were restless and refused to follow the old seminary ways. Their demands—following those of the student revolutionaries across the country—became more and more strident. I tried to swim with the radical tide. I led a seminarian protest against a ghastly display at the Museum of Science and Industry in which children could machine-gun Viet Cong invading a Vietnamese village. I invited the Chicago Seven (radicals who were tried for their provocative protests at the Democratic Convention) to speak at the seminary. They were irreverent and extreme, just what the students wanted.

With students and other faculty of the seminary, I went on a long bus ride to a protest march in Washington. It was massive. But what shocked me was that the majority of the marchers were not only against the war, they were against America. They were cheering for North Viet Nam to win—Ho, Ho, Ho Chi Min, Ho Chi Min! As we neared the Washington Monument we passed a tent city of protestors. Wafts of marijuana smoke floated upward.

Jugs of wine were stashed before the tent openings. Half-clad couples were having sex on the lawn. Wow. What had I gotten myself into? I was having grave doubts whether I could continue in the radical role I was trying to play. My outer life began to be in sharp conflict with my inner. Could I continue with any sort of integrity?

A few weeks later I attended a rally in the university neighborhood. Protestor after protestor rose to give impassioned pleas for revolutionary action to liberate their own particular oppressed group. They would finish their screed with: "Power to the People!" I watched with amazement. Walking home that evening it occurred to me that if power really were grasped by the people, the first victims of backlash would be the protesters. Moreover, I thought, instead of the revolution they sought they would get Richard Nixon, who would decisively win the election of 1972. I was right.

The next day I went into Dean Sherman's office and told him that he would soon hear surprising things from me in the classroom, in my writings, and from the students. I had come to the conclusion that the revolution was not for me. It was time to be honest with myself. My own assessment of America was far more positive than what I heard from the revolutionaries. Certainly some of that more benign interpretation was due to my own experience of growing up in America. But it was also a refusal to join the "revolution" because of its own craziness and extremity; common sense led me to a more measured stance.

These changes in political and economic opinion, which often led to feelings of isolation, were accompanied by a return to a classical view of the church as the bearer of the Gospel. I finally came to the conclusion that the church as a vehicle of social transformation instrumentalized it and reduced its transcendent message to purely human efforts. In Lutheran lingo, my view of the church changed from a purveyor of the law—a human work—to the bearer of the Gospel, the divine work of God in Christ. Consequently, my teaching gradually moved in that direction, far less emphatic and passionate about the church's direct political involvement. I did experience remorse that I had so fully accepted my earlier view of the church and its mission, and have often wondered how many students I influenced who never returned to a more orthodox view of the church. In later years they perhaps became "social justice warriors," whose exertions are now often inimical to mine.

By the time of my first sabbatical at Hamburg University in 1971-72, I had a much more dialectical view of America. Phil Hefner and I, after many of evenings of conversation over beer in Hamburg locales, decided to write a book together that was, to us at least, a more honest and nuanced view of America. We called it *Defining America—A Christian Critique of the American Dream*. It came out in 1974, just in time for the American Bicentennial. It garnered lots of speaking and writing engagements for us. But, more importantly, it made a more convincing argument about the positives in the American project than that generally offered by American academics. More about that in the next chapter.

Soon thereafter I began reading with excitement an emerging group of neo-conservative writers—Irving Kristol, Norman Podhoretz, Michael Novak, Richard John Neuhaus, among them. I resonated with how Kristol described a neo-conservative: "a liberal who had been mugged by reality." Or better for me, a "wanna-be radical who had been mugged by reality." I strongly identified with these neo-cons' affirmation of the role of religion in society, their commitment to a constitutional republic coupled with a market economic system, their support for a strong and free civil society, their positive assessment of America, and their belief in a strong America with an active, positive role in the world.

Later in the 70s I wrote a book that critically defended the combination of constitutional democracy and market economic arrangements called *The Ethic of Democratic Capitalism—A Moral Reassessment*. Like Michael Novak's later *The Spirit of Democratic Capitalism*, its argument swam against the stream of the conventional opinions of religious intellectuals of the time, who were hostile toward capitalism and friendly toward democratic socialism. Its novelty brought lots of attention, about fifty reviews and even a picture and short review in *Newsweek*.

My turn toward political and economic conservatism did not serve me well at the Lutheran School of Theology as we moved into the 80s. My faculty colleagues were surprised by that turn, but encouraged me to teach from my new perspective. However, the activist students were appalled. I was on the wrong side of history politically, economically, and culturally. A small discontented group showed their displeasure by organizing a successful boycott of a class I was offering on capitalism and justice. I no longer felt as welcomed in the coffee shop of the seminary. Further, I had taught by then seventeen years at LSTC and wondered whether that would be my only job. We also were getting weary of urban living. Hyde Park was not a family-friendly section of town.

TEACHING AT ROANOKE COLLEGE: 1982-2012

Right when we were ready to look around, Norman Fintel, president of Roanoke College, approached me about taking a newly endowed chair at Roanoke College, as well as about organizing a center that would strengthen the college's Lutheran identity. He had raised money for both purposes. After a year's hesitation because of the timing of our children's schooling, we said "yes."

So off to Salem, Virginia, to a school and region about which we knew very little. But what a blessing it was. I was able to organize the Center for Religion and Society, teach Christian theology and ethics from an endowed chair, and as department chair recruit a first-rate bevy of professors. As a family we discovered a strongly religious and family atmosphere in Salem. We were able to sell our small town house in Chicago for enough money to buy an ample four-bedroom home in Salem that bordered a farm with red barns and fifty head of cattle. As I was cutting the lawn once I thought to myself. Only in America could I have such a house and such a job in such a beautiful part of the country.

My children and grandchildren have also benefitted greatly from the "open and gracious future" that America provides. Though I believe their future is more cluttered and challenging than it was for me, they have done well. They love their country.

I have taught for many years from my settled Lutheran/Niebuhrian perspective and have written a number of books that I will discuss later. Sabbaticals were particularly helpful in getting them done. I organized hundreds of events for the Center for Religion and Society that engaged Lutheran/Christian theology and ethics with the challenges of the day. After I ran the Center for thirty years, Roanoke College renamed it in my honor in 2012. I will have much more to say about my time at Roanoke College in the next chapter.

I have written innumerable articles, editorials, and letters to the editor about public issues over the years. Most were for local papers, but a few got into *The Los Angeles Times* and *The Philadelphia Inquirer*. I was a writer on public affairs for *The Cresset*, Valparaiso University's review of literature, the arts, and public affairs, for twenty years. My occasional writings were gathered into a book published by Concordia Press called *Reasonable Ethics—A Christian Approach to Social, Economic, and Political Concerns* (2005). So, besides being a responsible citizen—abiding by the law, being self-reliant and self-governing, voting—I have made most of my contributions as a citizen by performing my role as a minor public intellectual. I belong to the Republican Party but have not participated vigorously, though I give it and its candidates modest monetary contributions. Mainly, however, my role has been as a commentator on public affairs.

Another American trait exemplified in my life has been my love of athletics. My father was a fine athlete—especially in baseball—and I grew up throwing the ball and watching live athletic competitions from the earliest time I can remember. When television became available watching games was even more persistent. An episode from my pre-teen years sticks out: Before we got TV, my father took me to a tavern below our apartment to watch Sunday afternoon pro football, which was just then beginning its ascent. Black players—Tank Younger, Marion Motley—were being introduced. Racist remarks in the tavern abounded, but my Dad said: "Don't pay any attention to those nasty words, Bobby; blacks are wonderful athletes and they will enrich the sport immensely." Dad was prophetic. He was also anti-Semitic and anti-Catholic. Go figure.

I played the traditional American sports through college and continued playing pick-up basketball for many years, but in my mid-20s discovered a new (to me) sport: tennis. I fell in love with it and played intensely from my mid-20s on. I tried to get my sons involved but they soon chose soccer. I have had many fine partner-friends and got good enough to be regionally ranked and win many tournaments. Sometimes, however, I think I was too intense about sports ... too American. I fear that my athletic commitments shown through stronger to our kids and grandkids than did my religious ones. But finally, I tell myself, with some degree of rationalization, that they are responsible for their choices in life.

2012-

After leaving employment at the college I have continued there as an unpaid Research Associate in the Department of Religion and Philosophy. I am writing these memoirs from my campus office. Right after leaving the employ the college I was recruited by the new Institute of Lutheran Theology to teach in their online M.Div. program. So back to seminary teaching I went. The technology was easier to master than I thought. I get to teach students—most of them mature adults—who have a strong desire to serve as ordained pastors. I teach two courses: Christian

Ethics and Christian Sexual Ethics, as well as an independent study now and then on the theological interpretation of film. I continue to lecture and write, but more of that later.

During all this time my political orientation—conservative—has provided the settled set of political convictions for the rest of my life, though the meaning of "conservative" is increasingly muddled. The former *Weekly Standard* was my kind of journal, as is *National Review*, which is more classically conservative. Add to those two journals *Commentary* and *First Things*, and you have a good sense of "where I am coming from." However, conservatism's positive assessment of America has not shielded me from real worries. Most of my worries are about the culture—the system of meanings and values that guide our country. Both politics and law are located downstream from the culture. The guidance system of the Judeo-Christian culture of post-war years has become weaker. It has been fractured into many sub-cultures, some of them hostile to the role of religion in public life. Further, the emergence of the "utilitarian and expressive individualism" that Robert Bellah, in his *Habits of the Heart* warned about, has undermined much of what was left of our common culture. The Marxist suspicion of inherited cultural norms as inherently oppressive has led the progressive elite—especially in our universities—to apply the "hermeneutic of suspicion" to them. Though that elite generally lives conventionally, it will not defend traditional norms to the larger culture. Its obsession with "diversity" and "inclusion" results in a moral relativism that confuses and divides rather than clarifies and unites.

The undermining of a common culture has led to the emergence of identity politics (only the very strong can be consistent individualists) and its attendant political correctness (a sort of leftist authoritarianism). Our country has become polarized and increasing decadent. Electronic communications—and the young's immersion in them—seem to exacerbate those negatives. Such conditions created an atmosphere in which a man such as Donald Trump could be elected President. (Years before his election, I used him as an example of extreme "utilitarian individualism" in one of my books!) That eventuality has strongly tested the political loyalties of many a Republican conservative, including me. Yet, in spite of all his and its faults, I stick with the Trump administration insofar as it presses forward a conservative agenda. I am especially concerned about the judiciary and its stance toward religious freedom. On that front the Trump administration has done well.

I worry about poor African-Americans and the struggling white working class. Many of those struggling have lost a clear and strong marriage and family ethic—partly because of the progressive elite's failure to support it—in the midst of great economic challenges, which have also played havoc with wholesome family life. I pray for a religious renewal in this country, one that would reach those poor sectors of our population. I have little clue how that revival will come about. Right now there seems little likelihood of that happening, though perhaps at the onset of the 19th century Christians had similar doubts about where and how to begin the Second Great Awakening. But the Spirit caught them up and energized their efforts so that they succeeded to a remarkable degree.

Nevertheless, all this said, I still thank the Lord that he threw me into an existence with all the particularities I have mentioned: my parents, my locations, my faith, my country, my time in history. I say: Thanks be to God! And not least of that gratitude is for my country, which offered me great opportunities and many open doors. The American dream has been real for me. I hope this chapter has shown how I have savored it.

Bob with faculty of Rock Island Campus of Lutheran School of Theology, 1967

As supply pastor, before decision to remain lay, 1966

Bob leading demonstration at the Museum of Science and Industry in Chicago, 1968

Cover of *The Lutheran* featuring Bob's move to Roanoke College, 1982

Lecturing at Roanoke College, 1994

Brochure for the Roanoke College Center for Religion and Society, 1983

Center Event– "Germany and the USA: Signals of Danger and Hope," 1985
(from left: Norman Fintel, Henry Fowler, Michael Naumann,
Walter Stoessel, Wolfhart Pannenberg, and Helmut Schmidt)

Center Event– "Celebration of Liberty," 1987
(from left: Bob, Martin Marty, Freeman Sleeper, Edward Albee,
Norman Fintel, James Kilpatrick, and William Hill)

Center Event– Poster for
N.T. Wright lecture, 2007

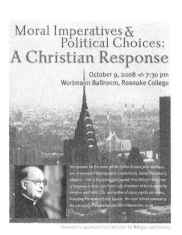

Center Event– Poster for Richard John
Neuhaus' last public lecture, 2008

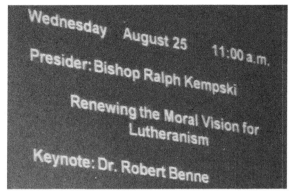
"New Directions in Lutheranism," Upper Arlington Lutheran Church, 2010

Bob lecturing at the "New Directions in Lutheranism" event

Carl Braaten, Bob, and Gerald McDermott at Bob's Festschrift Celebration, 2010

The crowd at the Festschrift Lecture is entertained by Carl Braaten

President Maxey, Bob and Joanna at a Crumley Lecture,
at which the Center was renamed in Bob's honor, 2012

Son Philip, Granddaughter Linnea, and Bob
in front of Martin Luther statue, Roanoke College, 2016

BRAATEN-BENNE LECTURES IN THEOLOGY
SCHEDULE

Tuesday, August 6

1:00 p.m.	Opening Prayer	Grand Ballroom
1:10 p.m.	Introduction and Greetings The Rev. Ron Hoyum, Chair The Rev. John Bradosky, Bishop	
1:15 p.m.	Lecture I: The Holy Spirit and Christian Life Dr. Robert Benne	
2:30 p.m.	Lecture II: How the Holy Spirit Disappeared in Lutheranism The Rev. Dr. Paul Hinlicky	
3:45 p.m.	Break	
4:10 p.m.	Lecture III: The Work of the Holy Spirit in the New Testament The Rev. Dr. Craig Keener	
5:30 p.m.	Dinner on your own; free evening	

Wednesday, August 7

8:00 a.m.	Opening Prayer	Grand Ballroom
8:15 a.m.	Lecture IV: The Holy Spirit and Salvation Dr. Matthew Levering	
9:30 a.m.	Lecture V: The Holy Spirit and the Stuff of Life The Rev. Dr. Derek Nelson	
10:45 a.m.	Break	
11:00 a.m.	Speaker's Forum	

Schedule from brochure for the Braaten-Benne Lecture, 2019

CHAPTER FOUR
MY CALLING AS A PRACTICAL THEOLOGIAN

This final chapter is the one most appropriate for a memoir, which is supposed to cover one specific aspect of the writer's life. As befits an autobiography, though, I have covered chronologically three other callings of my life—marriage and family; church, and life in America. Altogether, the four chapters really constitute an autobiography. But since the title of the book bears the word "memoirs," this last chapter will be the longest, and will perhaps be the one that readers turn to after they've read the preface and introduction.

In earlier chapters I have covered most of the significant public and private events of my life, but have not focused on my intellectual development and contributions as a Christian teacher and author. Teaching and writing practical theology have comprised my life's work, my vocation. Of course, those historical events cannot be separated from my thinking, teaching, and writing, so they will make their appearance again, hopefully without too much repetition. I will take up the story at the point of my intellectual awakening in college.

COLLEGE AND GRADUATE SCHOOL: 1959-1965

Having a new professor of religion, Allan Hauck, at Midland College in my senior year (1958-59) was a real blessing. As I mentioned earlier, he had us read Reinhold Niebuhr's *An Interpretation of Christian Ethics* in our required course in Christian ethics. I was captivated by Niebuhr's application of Christian theological ethics to economics and politics. For the first time the public relevance of the Christian faith came alive for me. Christianity was more than a private conviction, confined to the church, home, and individual heart. I read further in Niebuhr plus a bit of Kierkegaard, which gave me enough intellectual fire-power to write winning applications for a Fulbright Fellowship to Germany and a Woodrow Wilson Fellowship to the University of Chicago Divinity School.

During the time at Erlangen University in Germany (1959-60) I learned the basics of Lutheran theology—lectures by Paul Althaus—and Lutheran history—seminars with Wilhelm Maurer, but I must admit that I didn't work at either in a disciplined way. What interested me most was the course in Christian ethics offered by Walter Kuenneth, a rather heroic Lutheran ethicist who had been under house arrest during the Nazi era. He offered a good ground-work in the central themes of Lutheran ethics—two kingdoms, law and gospel, church and state, and vocation.[6]

That "Lutheran" year in Erlangen was good preparation for my entry into the University of Chicago Divinity School

---

6. While we did have luminaries teaching at Erlangen, a group of us longed for contact with the "really big guys"—Bultmann, Barth, and the Brunners. So we traveled to Heidelberg to hear the Brunners, to Basel to hear Barth, and to Marburg to hear and converse with Rudolph Bultmann, who invited us to his study for coffee and pastries...and pipe smoking. One of our group was a very conservative Wisconsin Synod Lutheran who thought Bultmann was a heretic. We knew he would pose an embarrassing question during our lengthy conversation with Bultmann. Finally, he blurted (in German): is it true, Professor Doctor Bultmann, that your theology is without God or eternity? Bultmann drew a long puff and calmly said: "I wouldn't say that; next question please." We all relaxed a bit.

in the fall of 1960. The dominant intellectual tradition at the Divinity School was process theology, with a bit of "empirical" theology thrown in. Alfred North Whitehead, Charles Hartshorne, and Henry Nelson Wieman were the leading lights. Key faculty represented those intellectual streams. Many students were influenced by their versions of liberal theology, i.e., updating the Christian faith to conform to modern thought-forms. Generally that meant jettisoning traditional Christianity with its doctrines of the Trinity, Incarnation, and Resurrection.

Yet, this was also the hey-day of neo-orthodox theology—Reinhold Niebuhr, Emil Brunner, Karl Barth, and Paul Tillich were also represented among the interests of the faculty, as was the de-mythologizing effort of Rudolph Bultmann. With all these options available and enthusiastically promoted, one might rightly guess that there was exciting intellectual jousting among the faculty and the students. There were many theological conferences and public conversations where the faculty went at it. I was mesmerized by the academic weight and intensity of the debates. I particularly remember a stunning performance at our opening convocation by Nathan Scott, an African-American, who spoke in paragraph-long sentences without a hitch.[7]

---

7. One of the great benefits of a Chicago education at that time was exposure to some of the great theologians of the era. Barth, Thielicke, Tillich, and Nygren lectured or resided at the Divinity School. One member of the Swedish Lundensian school, Ragnar Bring, came to teach courses in Luther. His lecture hall was full for his first lecture, but he was not fluent in English and his lectures were halting and simple. After two lectures only a couple of us were attending. Crestfallen, he told the dean that he was so embarrassed that he would return to Sweden immediately. The dean confided the sad news to Gerald Christianson and me. We decided to save Bring from disgrace by ensuring that at least five students were present for his classes. We created a schedule that indicated when each in our circle of friends had to attend to make up a decent class showing. The gambit was successful. Professor Bring, perhaps sensing something unusual was going on, was visibly relieved and concluded the course. My wife and I developed a friendship with the Brings and visited them in Sweden when we were on sabbatical.

The students were bright and highly motivated; they joined in the fray. Theological ideas mattered. That meant you had to stake out a position and be able to defend it in classrooms, the lively Swift Hall coffee shop, or Jimmy's Woodlawn Tap, where you could get a large pitcher of beer for a dollar and visit a rest room whose walls were filled with erudite graffiti. It was an exciting time; I have never known such pervasive, lively, intellectual interaction.

In order to hold my ground, though, I had to appropriate Lutheran theology at a lot deeper level than I had grasped earlier, far deeper than I had picked up in Erlangen. I read the great Scandinavians—Aulen, Nygren, Wingren—and the American Lutherans—Forell and Lazareth. After a year or so of immersion in those thinkers I could defend my orthodox Lutheranism. Moreover, I wasn't alone in the intellectual fisticuffs. There was a Lutheran Theological Fellowship that featured such impressive students as Robert Wilken, Phil Hefner, and Paul Sponheim. They were far ahead of me intellectually, but they served as models for us younger aspirants.

During my first year at the Divinity School I came to the conclusion that my interests and gifts drew me to "practical theology," the application of theological ethics to societal issues: politics, economics, and culture. What excited me was the study of the role of religion in various sectors of public life. The courses I took in Ethics and Society stirred me more than those in theology. Moreover, as I listened to the many debates featuring systematic theologians, I often thought that they got too tied up in highly subtle—and frankly, irrelevant—topics and distinctions. I knew, of course, that reliable theology was extremely important, but doubted that it meant delving into so many esoteric subtleties. Such efforts certainly were not my cup of tea. So I steered toward what I thought were far more relevant pursuits. That meant that I would be applying a given theology—Lutheran/Niebuhrian—to the public world rather than trying to construct my own.

Throughout that first year I felt pretty inferior to the other students, most of whom were seminary grads from prestigious schools. The few who came directly from undergraduate schools seemed far more sophisticated than I. They were from Yale or Harvard; I was from Midland College. They posed questions like "What is your hermeneutic of history?" in casual conversation. I thought I might as well make plans to transfer to the Lutheran seminary in suburban Maywood when I flunked out of Chicago. (At our fall orientation banquet at the University's Quadrangle Club, Dean Jerald Brauer told us that half of us wouldn't be at the University next fall.)

But a powerful moment of "common grace" made me feel a lot better about myself. Our first year featured survey courses in Old Testament and New Testament. The New Testament course was taught in the spring by Markus Barth, son of the famous Karl. For the term paper in his course, I wrote on "Paul and Mysticism." I worked very hard on it. After he had graded them, he called each of us into his office for a consultation on our paper. A group of us waited nervously in the third-floor common room outside his office. I was called in last. Upon entry he said to me: "I fear for your soul, Mr. Benne." Yikes. I thought I had done so badly that he was worried that I would jump from the nearest window when I got the bad news. But he followed up by saying: "You wrote such a fine paper that I have given you an A plus and I fear that you will become too arrogant toward your fellow students." After that I didn't feel so subordinate.

The University of Chicago tradition was to read a few great texts deeply rather than read many texts superficially. So we read classic texts in each of the seven areas in which we had to pass comprehensive exams. Engaging those seven areas—Constructive Theology, Old Testament and New Testament, Church History, Religion and Personality, Religion and Art, History of Religions, and Ethics and Society—was an incredible learning experience. In the year-long course in Ethics and Society, my preferred field, we were expected by our professor, Al Pitcher, to pick a theologian and really "get inside" his thought. I had already been introduced to Reinhold Niebuhr so I eagerly delved into *The Nature and Destiny of Man*, as well as his ample writings on theology and politics. I read him so closely that I could "think like Niebuhr," and got A's on my papers employing his thought.

That was very useful because it tied into the great enthusiasms of the "liberal idealism" that I described in my chapter on being an American. Niebuhr was very helpful in giving a theological rationale for the civil rights movement, community organization activities, and the efforts to eradicate poverty. Each of those initiatives were powerfully presented to us by Al Pitcher, who not only gave us an enthusiastic account of them in class, but was actually deeply involved in all of them. He got us excited; he got us involved. Great changes were afoot in America and the mainline churches were fully immersed in them.

Given the power and excitement of these movements, it was easy to view the churches as instruments of social transformation. Without denying my newly formulated Lutheranism, I put that on back burner for the sake of a Niebuhrian-fueled involvement in social transformation. The traditional functions of the church—preaching, teaching, worship, personal formation—came in second to the great need for the church to participate in these movements. The most popular theological book of the time, Harvey Cox's *The Secular City,* argued as much when it came out in 1965. Cox maintained that God is involved in public, political action for justice and peace. That is where he should be found, not in the private activities in church buildings. Get out of the church and into the streets! I became a "social justice warrior" before the term had been coined.

THE LUTHERAN SCHOOL OF THEOLOGY AT CHICAGO: 1965-1982

When I began teaching at the seminary level in 1965, Cox's book, coupled with Michael Harrington's *The Other America*, provided a potent teaching combination for me. Since I had had Hannah Arendt as a professor at the University of Chicago, I also added her *The Human Condition*, with its emphasis on "action" (*vita activa*) as the quintessential human enterprise, to the mix. Moreover, one of my teachers, Gibson Winter—who was to become my doctor father—had published *The Suburban Captivity of the Churches* in 1961 in which he argued that the churches had to overcome that "captivity" by taking a much wider view of their ministry. They had to join the struggle for urban renewal and racial justice. Two years later his *New Creation as Metropolis* proposed longitudinal parishes that encompassed suburban and urban sections of the city. Such a provision would insure that churches would grapple with inner-city and racial issues rather than escape them. Churches would then transcend their myopic obsession with "religious" activities and get to the real world of social transformation.

Those exciting books provided the script for my early teaching at the Rock Island campus of the Lutheran School of Theology. Backed up by my Niebuhrian emphasis on the need for power to the powerless, that script was as energizing for the excellent students fresh from the Augustana Synod churches and colleges as it was for me. They caught my excitement and many decided they wanted to become urban ministers. As previously noted, one of them, Rick Deines, became our pastor when I began teaching at the new Chicago campus of the Lutheran School of Theology at Chicago.

While I certainly attended chapel and church, my focus was on the exciting social movements of the time. It stirred up enough excitement among the Rock Island students that the new administration of LSTC decided to make room for me at the new campus in Hyde Park, Chicago. I was offered the position of Assistant Professor of Church and Society and moved back with my family to Chicago in 1967 after the two years in Rock Island.

This strong affirmation of my teaching finally persuaded me that my calling in the church was to be a teacher and writer.

Though I did quite a bit of supply preaching in the Rock Island area, I did not feel drawn to the ordained ministry. Leading worship services did not excite me and I had few gifts for spontaneous prayer. While I could think of a thousand topics to talk about as a teacher, I could think of few items to pray about as a pastor. I didn't think I should become ordained simply for the tax-free housing allowance. Moreover, the seminary was no longer requiring that its faculty be ordained with some parish experience, as it did of old. So it seemed natural to give up my long-held plans for seminary training and subsequent ordination. Besides, I loved teaching. I got strong affirmation of my teaching style, much of it an imitation of my old mentor, Al Pitcher. Further, I published an article in the seminary journal that was well received. That gave me a thirst for writing for journals. My first article of note—"The Limits of Power and the Need for Persuasion"—appeared in *The Christian Century* in 1968. These successes confirmed my decision to remain a lay teacher and writer.

The new Chicago campus, featuring a stunning new academic building, drew many students who were as excited about those accelerating social movements as my Rock Island students were. I taught roomfuls of ninety students in my course on church and society. I called the church to activism and I summoned these clergy-to-be to lead it in that direction. As students were sent into the new "teaching parish" program of the seminary, I tried to get them to press the social ministry committees of the Chicagoland churches to which they were assigned to get involved in the great struggles of the time. I railed against "mere charity" and charged the students to get the local churches to "attack the structures of injustice in society." Truth be told, not many local parishes were interested; they persisted in their retrograde Lutheran commitment to charity within and outside their congregations. They did not want to plunge headlong into social action. Students were discouraged. We blamed "Lutheran quietism" for the churches' lassitude. For the most part, those churches just didn't do what I thought they should do. They were too mired in what I thought was the geriatric *status quo*.

About this time I received a grant from the Lutheran Church in America to organize an Institute for Metropolitan Ministries (IMM). One of its first actions was to offer a course called "Social Transformation," which was offered through the Chicago Cluster of Theological Schools, a consortium of five or six seminaries in the University of Chicago neighborhood. The course was taught by church and society professors of the various schools, including a militant nun, Marjorie Tuite, from a newly arrived order of Catholic sisters. I also arranged for chief organizer Leon Finney of The Woodlawn Organization (TWO) to offer courses in community organization at the seminary. The TWO was an Alinsky-style community organization that engaged in many controversial actions to press the University of Chicago and the city of Chicago to take seriously the needs of the poor community of Woodlawn, right south of the university itself. These courses drew activist students to this divisive approach, which demanded that churches as churches join the community organization. This tended to upset many churches, whose lay people resisted the idea of their church joining a conflict-oriented community organization.

I was aware that most of my teaching and the IMM's work was focused on institutional concerns and activism, getting churches to join in the fray. But I thought the Institute needed to pay more attention to "personal transformation," which, after all, was a central concern of the church. That concern seemed to be addressed powerfully by the programs of the Ecumenical Institute, a venture of radical Methodists who offered introductory courses to the Christian faith (Religious Studies I), workshops on anti-racism, and training in community transformation. I was particularly interested in Religious Studies I, which employed some fascinating pedagogical tools to communicate an existentialist version of the Christian faith.

Religious Studies I consisted of stirring lectures on God, Christ, the Holy Spirit and the Church. Each lecture was combined with a "directed discussion" of short essays by the heavy-hitting theologians of the time: Bultmann, Tillich, and H. Richard Niebuhr. Participants saw how key doctrines were applicable to the existential realities of their lives. This was reinforced by applying the doctrines to a showing of Rod Serling's *Requiem for a Heavyweight*, a gritty movie that could be interpreted through the categories the course had just conveyed. "RSI," as we called it, was a powerful pedagogical tool, far more effective than any of the approaches taught in the religious education courses in the seminaries.

From my first encounter with the course, though, I thought it was excessively existentialist and had to be "Lutheranized," which I worked at. Conversations with my colleague (and tennis partner), Carl Braaten, were very helpful in that process. Soon I began gathering a team of professors from LSTC who could offer such a course to the urban and suburban Lutheran churches that needed to be energized in their Christian beliefs and convictions. After such renewal perhaps they would be more likely to lead their churches into the social movements raging all around them.

The work of the IMM was expanding and it needed full-time leadership, which I could not supply. So we—the Steering Committee of the IMM—recruited pastor William Lesher from St. Luke's, a Lutheran congregation on the northwest side of Chicago. Bill was already deeply involved in the Ecumenical Institute's efforts at church and neighborhood renewal so he was right in line with what we were already doing. Further, he was a man of great energy and determination. He took up the tasks of the IMM so quickly and effectively that he was recruited to be president of the Lutheran seminary in Berkeley, California, after three or four years of work with the IMM at LSTC. After only a few years at Berkeley, he returned as president of LSTC for a long tenure.

Over time we did scores of retreats with church councils and other groups within the Lutheran churches of the Chicago area. The courses went over very well but the week-end efforts—in addition to our regular teaching jobs—were exhausting. Further, we not only offered this lively pedagogical approach to the churches, we offered it to the students at LSTC instead of the rather pedestrian offerings in religious education. A whole generation of students was taught an effective approach to teaching the faith.

I appropriated many of the techniques and teachings of that course for my own work. It provided the theological backbone of my first book, *Wandering in the Wilderness—Christians and the New Culture*, which was written on my first sabbatical in 1971-72 and published in 1972. The short book used this "existentialist/Lutheran" theological approach to make sense of the irruptions of the mid- and late-60s. In retrospect, I was far too uncritical about what was happening in those years, but the full impact of the 60s (1965-75) was yet to come fully upon me. Only my hind-sight is 20-20. But at least the book indicated by its title that Christians were trying to find their way in a rapidly changing and confusing world.

My Ph.D. dissertation was accepted in 1970, five years after I had passed my doctoral exams. I had worked on it only in summers, a painful and slow way of completing academic requirements. I received that degree in March of that year. The dissertation dealt with a theological critique of four theories of mass society: those of William Kornhauser, C. Wright Mills, Lloyd Warner, and Hannah Arendt. "Theory of mass society" was an important concept in the 50s and 60s. It sought to understand the malaise of society that resulted from the erosion of "intermediate groups," i.e. those institutions standing between the individual and large-scale political and economic organizations. My dissertation was caught up in what some academics called "the University of Chicago disease," which by that they meant a "paralysis of analysis." My doctor father, Gibson Winter, kept pressing me to go beyond analysis to a more constructive argument, which I finally did. I argued more directly that the social movements of the early 60s were a response to and an important way to overcome mass society.

The "social transformation" in which I was caught up in my graduate and early teaching years was part and parcel of the liberal idealism of those years. It was this optimistic social project that I was exhorting the churches to join, often (at least in my teaching) at the expense of the more traditional roles and functions of the church. But that emphasis was about to end, thanks to the radical upheavals of the 60s.

As I chronicled in the chapter on life in America, the 60s from 1965 onward demolished that optimistic liberal idealism—basically reformist in character—and replaced it with revolutionary spirit and movements. I will not repeat the story I told in chapter three. Suffice it to say that I decided that I couldn't go along with that revolutionary spirit when I was confronted with what it really turned out to be. Building upon an exceedingly negative view of America and its role in the world, it agitated for revolutionary change. I could go along with neither. I catalogued some of my experiences that led to disgust and disaffiliation in chapter three.

So, after grieving over what status and clout I would lose as I abandoned the role of "house radical" at LSTC, I finally had the courage to get off the revolutionary train. There were persuasive voices that helped me in that transition after I, like they, had been "mugged by reality." Of course, among them were the New York, Jewish, neo-conservative intellectuals. Irving Kristol, Daniel Bell, and Norman Podhoretz were particularly influential. Richard John Neuhaus, a new Lutheran friend, and fellow traveler in many ways, was the most important Christian voice that helped me find my new road. Michael Novak, particularly his positive evaluation of capitalism, was also informative. Another influential stream were the writings of University of Chicago economists, especially those of Milton Friedman, as well as extended conversations with another of my tennis partners, Eugene Fama, who later received a Nobel Prize for his work. They demolished the flimsy economic ideas I had gained from reading only Karl Marx and John Kenneth Galbraith in graduate school.

They made me take another look at economics, especially those thinkers that appreciated market economic systems.

Perhaps now aligning more coherently with my own appropriation of American history and experience, I was leaving "revolution" behind in favor of a more conservative orientation in politics, economics, and culture. With regard to the latter category—culture—I was moving toward a more positive assessment of American culture by the early 70s. I had seen enough of the radical critique of America. The Left had become America haters. During the sabbatical year of 1971-72 I finished *Wandering in the Wilderness* early and was looking for another writing project for the rest of the year. As it happened, both the Hefner and the Benne families had planned to spend that sabbatical year together in Hamburg, Germany. After becoming acquainted with Helmut Thielicke when he spent a year at the University of Chicago in 1963, we were invited by that eminent theologian and preacher to spend our sabbatical year at Hamburg University.

After both Phil and I had finished our initial projects, we began to plan another one: a more nuanced and appreciative interpretation of America, especially its underlying myth. I was assigned to define that myth, the American Dream, while both Phil and I agreed to reflect on its ambiguous nature. It wasn't hard for me to define the Dream because generations of my family had experienced it. It exhorted everyone to "shake free from the limits of the past, engage in a struggling ascent while playing by the rules, and be greeted by a gracious and open future." We argued that the vast majority of Americans were shaped by the Dream and had achieved it in some fashion. But we also reflected on some of the ambiguities of the Dream itself: it left an awful lot of human wreckage in the past as it strove for the future; some people were excluded from the dream, people often did not play by the rules, and for many people the future did not greet their efforts with open arms. The title of the book catches that sort of dialectical approach: *Defining America: A Christian Critique of the American Dream*.

We got the book published by Fortress in time for the celebration of the American Bicentennial. Because we demurred from a radical critique and offered a more nuanced interpretation of American life, we were invited to write and lecture widely. Sometimes we took blistering criticism from those who thought we were "selling out," but more often we were greeted more kindly by those who wished for a more appreciative interpretation of the Dream and how it has fared. The book sold well enough that we wrote a study guide to help churches and college students grapple with contending views of American life after 200 years of nationhood.

In the mid-70s I found myself at odds with my teachers, Gibson Winter and Al Pitcher. They had organized a "Seminar on the American Future" in which ethics professors from the Cluster schools participated. As the 60s unfolded, both of them became more pessimistic and negative about the American project. But I, along with a professor from the neighboring Chicago Theological Seminary, Widick Schroeder, were moving in the opposite direction. So, while the seminar featured lively debate about American society, it more or less soured my relationship with my earlier mentors. They thought I had betrayed our academic calling as critics.

My conversion from radicalism to neo-conservatism in politics and economics led me to write a book on those subjects that garnered wide attention. Annoyed at how easily the combination of constitutional democracy and market economic arrangements was being dismissed by intellectuals in both society and church, I vowed to make a counter-argument. My sabbatical in 1978-79 was given over fully to work on that project. This time I elected to go to Cambridge with my family of six (!), where I not only could find ample research material but also plenty of opportunities to bounce my argument off interested professors at that great university. Most of them, of course, were aghast that anyone—especially a Christian—would make a defense of capitalism.

I made my case for a combination of democracy and market economic arrangements in a book entitled *The Ethic of Democratic Capitalism: A Moral Reassessment*, which, though I had finished its manuscript in 1979, did not get published until 1982. It drew immediate attention because it went counter to the conventional commitment of religious intellectuals to democratic socialism. Reviews of the book appeared in around fifty journals, newspapers, and magazines, including *Time* and *Newsweek*. My photo even appeared in the latter. Michael Novak came along a few months later with his *The Spirit of Democratic Capitalism*. While his marketing and sales were far superior to mine, the reviews of his book were generally less positive than mine, mainly because my book was a "critical" assessment of "democratic capitalism," while his was more a paean of praise. Interestingly, when he found out that my book was going to hit the market earlier than his, he demanded—quite insistently—that I change the title of my book since it was so similar to what he would be giving his. However, my publisher, Fortress, had already registered the title and received an ISBN number; there was no turning back. Sadly, Novak never seemed to forgive me for "beating him to the punch," even though that did harm neither to his sales nor the attention that he received from many quarters. But I admit that I still admire his book about sports.

In my book of disputed title I first established that there was such a thing as "workably competitive markets," a reality that many critics denied. Then I showed how such markets actually functioned to provide many goods that any flourishing society needed, not only material goods but also other features: economic freedom as a basis of other freedoms, discretionary income that enabled a flourishing civil society, and enough economic autonomy that enabled governments to be limited. But, despite the virtues of market economic arrangements, I argued that constitutional democratic governments had to play an indispensable role in the pursuit of justice. I critically employed John Rawls' theory of justice to offer guiding principles for just policies. Finally, I argued that for democracy and markets to operate constructively, they needed to be undergirded by a strong and healthy culture, which was supplied by a robust civil society and threatened by the "cultural contradictions of capitalism" itself. In short, I offered an "ambiguously positive" case for the combination of democracy and capitalism, most likely the best arrangement for advanced industrial societies.

The book brought me many speaking and writing opportunities. One major lecture was offered in 1979 before the book was published. I was invited to speak at the Nobel Conference held annually at Gustavus Adolphus College. The conference theme that year was the "Future of the Market Economy" and featured a number of distinguished economists. My talk was entitled "Ought the Market Economy Have a Future?" to which I responded with firm affirmation. This surprised those who nominated me to speak because they thought I would offer the typical religious intellectual's denunciation of capitalism. Often I lectured to groups that more or less used me as a foil to make their case for democratic socialism. At other times I spoke to friendly crowds who were surprised to hear any good words about capitalism coming from a theological ethicist. Throughout the 80s the debate among ethicists about competing political economies was hot and heavy. It came to a temporary end with the fall of communism in the late 80s. I then was able puckishly to claim that my book was so persuasive that it brought down "real existing socialism." Once the socialist and communist leaders read it they knew the game was over.

If my political and economic "conversion" was rather dramatic, so was my turn to more traditional notions about the identity and mission of the church. I had invested much in getting students, pastors, and churches to join in "social transformation." But with the emergence of 60s radicalism, there was little hope of getting Lutheran churches to participate in "revolutionary praxis." Moreover, I no longer believed in the direction the radicals had taken the "movement," or in the direction I had been trying to move the church.

It was back to the drawing board with regard to my teaching about the mission of the church and the Christian life. With regard to the former, I backed off the notion that the church is primarily an instrument of social transformation. Rather, I began teaching that through its traditional practices—preaching, sacraments, worship, teaching, learning—the church formed the kind of persons who would affect society profoundly in the long run. It was the indirect effects of the church that were most important to society. The disciples of Christ could be leaven and salt. Also, I quit impugning the charitable efforts of the church and was far more modest and realistic about what the church could and ought to do politically.

In the late 70s and early 80s I began to develop my own interpretation of Lutheranism's teaching on vocation—the calling of each Christian. I returned again to the work of Wingren and Forell to help me formulate my approach. This change of emphasis anchored my teaching in more traditional ecclesiology and theological ethics. It was a turn toward individual formation and discipleship after many years of focusing on "social transformation." That was a welcome turn for a minority of students at LSTC, but a disappointing—and boring—turn for the majority, who were strongly aligned with the Left. These left-wing students were even more upset by my critical appreciation of "democratic capitalism." Even though I was featured in several national magazines as a result of my work on democratic capitalism, that did not prevent the activist students at LSTC from venting their displeasure at my turn toward conservatism in politics and economics. They organized a successful boycott of my course on "Capitalism and Justice." I think it was the only course I ever offered that had to be cancelled.

Back to the early 70s. It was in this tumultuous time that one of my LSTC colleagues began preaching and teaching an apocalyptic theology that identified America as the whore of Babylon. The activist students loved it. But one very conservative faculty member didn't. He began sending anonymous "hate mail" of a vile but sophisticated sort to the activist theologian. Threats were made, which deeply disturbed the faculty and administration of the school. After all, this was a seminary. There were fairly accurate suspicions of whom might be sending the messages. When the suspected faculty member was on vacation over a break, the dean got legal permission to take a sample of the typing from the suspect's typewriter. Lo and behold, the typeset matched that of the hate mail. Soon thereafter the guilty faculty member was forced to apologize privately to the theologian and to leave the seminary quickly.

Another faculty member had a daughter who joined the Symbionese Liberation Army and was killed in a police shootout on the West Coast. Yet another lost a "foster-son" in a police raid on the "safe house" of a group of Black Panthers in Chicago. "Revolution" affected the seminary in many ways. I was not the only one flinching from its effects, which were in my case minor compared to others.

A good deal of the revolution was cultural, especially sexual. The sexual revolution of the 60s deeply affected the seminaries in the 70s. They were not immune to its excesses. We faculty heard rumors of illicit sexual shenanigans in the dorms, but pretty much tried to ignore the rumors. In fact, the seminary became known as a "gay friendly" school, perhaps because of its location and its reputation for being "on the cutting edge." Gays and lesbians came in considerable numbers. In the early 70s one lesbian "came out of the closet" and asked to be accepted in the M.Div. program, which prepared students for ordained ministry in the church. The academic dean, Frank Sherman, refused to take that step, which quieted down any sort of public agitation even though there were many gays in the pipeline. Though I had a number of gay advisees among the LSTC students, none of them would publicly "come out" after the dean's decision. Some remained single and made it into the ordained ministry. Others had "partners" on the side. Some died of AIDS.

The sexual revolution hit the Catholic seminaries in the Chicago Cluster of Theological Schools particularly hard. Like LSTC, the Catholic seminaries had a large influx of gay men. A gay subculture developed that probably harbored some of the priests charged with sexual misconduct in the 80s and 90s. The students at the Jesuit school were particularly active in finding ways to skirt the literal meaning of "chastity" and "celibacy." Others—heterosexual men—left the priesthood. Many seminarians jettisoned Catholic teachings on sexual ethics and embraced the "new morality." Even some Catholic faculty backed off traditional teaching.

Though I had some sympathy with the sexual revolution in its early stages, I reverted to a more traditional approach to sexual morality by the late 70s. The loosening of all restraints was leading to chaos in the sphere of personal morality, much like it was producing turbulence in the social and political spheres. Besides, it seemed to me that biblical and traditional Christian teachings on sexual ethics were quite clear. It now was time to re-affirm them in the classroom. I began teaching a course in Christian sexual ethics that had as its foil a new (1978) book by James Nelson entitled *Embodiment: An Approach to Sexuality and Christian Theology*. The book was a theological gloss on the sexual revolution. It had a chapter entitled "Sexual Salvation," which reveals something of its celebration of the new freedoms. It provided a good occasion to argue for a more classical approach, which I drew from Helmut Thielicke's *The Ethics of Sex*. Many students signed up for the course. From there on I aimed at defending Christian teachings where they were being—and continue to be—sharply attacked. I developed the course into a strong affirmation of traditional Christian ethics. I continue to teach the course—with many new readings—to the present day. Little did I anticipate that 30 years later my own church would depart from those traditional teachings.

With these multiple moves toward a more traditional politics, economics, culture, and, above all, theology, I felt less and less at home at the Lutheran School of Theology. There were other conservative faculty, but they kept a low profile. They encouraged me to continue on my new, but old, path. Other faculty were friendly and supportive; a few activist types were less so. Though there were many traditional Lutheran students, the vocal sector of the student body was actively hostile to my teaching. I was deemed to be on the wrong side of history on a number of fronts. Strong feminism was gaining traction at the seminary, initiating a relentless effort to change the language of worship. Many more women were entering the M. Div. program. Though I had been a strong supporter of women's ordination and advised—and defended—one of the first women ordinands of the seminary, I found the entering cohort more militant and more interested in pursuing a feminist agenda than committing to the mission of the church. The activist LSTC students were also deeply involved in the movement to divest from South Africa and boycott its goods. I thought the selective divestment strategy favored by Leon Sullivan was wiser, so I found myself in conflict with the activists on yet another issue.

I had been teaching at LSTC for fifteen years by 1980 and was wondering if I was going to have only one job my whole life. Our family of six was getting a bit restive about living in a small townhouse in Hyde Park. I felt out of synch with the seminary student body. A kind of malaise had set in. I was open to new and different ventures.

ROANOKE COLLEGE: 1982-

Providentially, a very attractive door opened. Norman Fintel, president of Roanoke College in Virginia, which I had scarcely heard of, came calling. He had a plan to draw the college closer to its Lutheran heritage, which he thought needed strengthening. He had been the chief executive for the American Lutheran Church's division of higher education. He knew what a robust Lutheran college looked like and feared that Roanoke's connection to its Lutheran tradition was in danger of a fatal weakening, as had happened at other eastern Lutheran colleges. He had raised money for an endowed chair in the Religion and Philosophy Department as well an endowment for a center that would enrichen the college's Christian credentials.

He was searching for a mid-career Lutheran who had already achieved something of a reputation. An LSTC student—Tim Swanson—whom I had taught in the early 70s was at that time the chaplain at Roanoke and recommended me. I had excellent conversations with Norman and his influential wife, Jo. Norm and I were fellow Nebraska Lutherans who shared a lot of convictions. I visited the beautiful campus and had interviews with faculty and students who shared Fintel's belief that Lutheran presence at the college should be strengthened. Moreover, the Religion and Philosophy Department had just experienced something of a scandal involving its chair and it needed new leadership badly. Its morale and reputation were in bad shape.

During the summer of 1981 I took the family to Salem, Virginia, where the college was located. We were all excited by the prospect of such a move. It was so different from our Chicago lives. Unfortunately, our children were at awkward moments in school; their lives would be badly disrupted were we to leave at that time. I regretfully declined Norm's offer and we battened down for more years in Chicago. A couple of weeks later, Norm called with this lovely news: "We will wait a year." Joanna and I quickly came to the conclusion that we should accept the offer. So we did.

It was difficult to leave faculty colleagues with whom I had worked since the inception of the new seminary in Chicago in 1967. I felt like I was jumping ship. I wanted counsel so I asked for advice from the aged Joseph Sittler, the revered Lutheran theologian/preacher, whom I had had as a professor at the Divinity School and who was retired in Hyde Park. I told him I felt like I was about to leave the "land of the living." He responded; "Benne, you will feel like you are dead for about three weeks, but then you will resurrect. If you think this is important for your family and for your career, do it." So we did.

A WAKE-UP CALL

When we got to Salem in the summer of 1982 Norm took me out to lunch. He said he wanted me to work on four things: 1. Build a first-rate Religion and Philosophy Department; 2. Organize and name the center for which an endowment had been raised; 3. Help to elevate the intellectual life on campus; 4. Find other ways to strengthen the college's relation to its Lutheran/Christian heritage. He said he would support me in these endeavors but could not be seen to favor me unduly. Further, he said: "do those things and don't talk about them." I took the latter to mean that if I were too public about my plans I would generate resistance.

I took him right. Resistance was soon to come, whether or not I was public about my plans. The first came after a full-blown feature—with pictures of our arriving family—was run in the *Roanoke Times* upon our arrival in Salem. (Salem and Roanoke are contiguous cities, and Roanoke College is in Salem.) The feature was written by the newspaper's well-meaning but unwary religion writer. During an interview with her I had mentioned how delightful it was to be in a smaller town that was family-oriented and religious, in contrast to the university neighborhood in Chicago in which we had lived. Further, I mentioned that my wife felt more comfortable in a traditional culture in which she could be a full-time mother without constantly having to justify why she did not work outside the home.

The religion writer captioned her article: "Theologian Flees the Big City for Salem" and then proceeded to make us sound as if we were anti-feminist and anti-urban. The article, of course, was read by the women professors of the college, who took that to mean that I was a kind of fundamentalist who wanted women "barefoot, pregnant, and in the kitchen," and thought that the city of Chicago was a dark den of sin. Not a good start at my new place of work.

Further, as I got to know more about the Roanoke College faculty I found that my initial impressions from "friendly" faculty and students whom I had met when first visiting the college were more than a bit skewed. Most faculty didn't care much about the college's religious heritage; some were eager to get rid of it. That came home to me as I got to know the department chairs, who met periodically. Three were overtly hostile to the college's religious heritage. One, who resented Norm's establishment of an endowed chair in religion, had some nice words for me when we met. "Oh," she said, dripping with sarcasm, "you're special." Another gave me a back-hand compliment by designating me "the most dangerous man on campus."

Five out of the eleven chairs were apathetic, which meant that they thought the current weak relation to the college's Lutheran heritage was "just right." Later, when we did make overt attempts to strengthen that heritage, I found out what "just right" meant. It meant that any effort to strengthen that relationship was met with fervent resistance. Three of the chairs were supportive of strengthening our connection to the church and the Christian heritage, but were most reluctant to voice their opinions. I had met them in my earlier interviews and mistakenly thought that all the department chairs had similar attitudes.

The faculty as a whole reflected the attitudes of the department chairs. There was little support for even talking about our relationship to our Lutheran heritage, let alone strengthening it. The college was on a slow movement to complete secularization. The hostility and apathy toward our Lutheran heritage was a powerful signal of that process. This was quite an awakening for me. Though I had visited many church-related colleges in the twenty-two years I had been away from Midland, I had no idea how powerful and extensive were the processes of secularization. The Midland I went to was overwhelmingly populated by Lutheran faculty and students. Roanoke had eight Lutherans among its ninety full-time faculty. Its student body ran at about eight percent Lutheran. Midland had required chapel; Roanoke had no chapel but a Sunday morning service that was sparsely attended. Midland's faculty was very supportive of Christian growth in the college's students. Roanoke's professors, except for a few, were apathetic. And there were no educators at Midland hostile to its close connection to its Christian heritage. Roanoke had a powerful minority of faculty who actually wanted to divorce the college from its Lutheran tradition. Of course, some of this had to do with location—the Southeast where there were few Lutherans versus the Midwest where there were plenty—but more had to do with a weak sense of purpose and the attendant failure to "hire for mission."

POSITIVE STEPS

This realization took me aback enough to want to understand the secularization process more fully before I made any efforts to push forward on Norm's fourth charge to me: think of ways to strengthen the college's Lutheran identity and mission. Meanwhile, all was not lost. Fintel had recognized the college's dangerous trajectory and made some gestures to impede that process, including hiring me to occupy an endowed chair, chair the department, and organize a center. Further, he invited the Virginia Synod headquarters to reside on the college campus in a lovely old building that had been the college's library. He hired a full-time church relations director, Kathryn Buchanan, and placed her in resource development where she proceeded to gather money for more endowed chairs in religion and scholarships for Lutheran students.

Another major step forward was Fintel's selection in 1984 of a new academic dean, Gerald Gibson, who not only was friendly to the Christian heritage of the college, but was willing to allow me as chair of the department of religion and philosophy to hire three new faculty. Those three—Ned Wisnefske (1985), Gerald McDermott[8] (1989), and Hans Zorn (1990)—joined Freeman

---

8. McDermott was a particularly important recruit. As a conservative evangelical at that time, he thought no mainline liberal college would hire him. I was impressed by him and persuaded the department to select him. Little did we know what an energetic and talented teacher, writer, and lecturer

Sleeper, who had moved from the deanship of the college to our department where he taught his specialty, biblical studies. Two older men had retired and the new acquisitions enabled us to offer a full panoply of theological courses: Bible, theology, ethics, church history, world religions, plus electives in those fields. The philosophy side of the department was bolstered by Zorn, who taught extensively in business ethics and religious philosophy.

The strength of the department soon attracted majors, particularly double majors: those who did one major in a secular field but wanted to pursue their religious interests. In a few years we were graduating a dozen or more majors a year, a huge contrast with the one lonely religion major we had when I arrived in 1982. This support from the dean—and the president's concurrence—enabled me to strengthen the department markedly. Later on we were able to add even more positions, including one filled by Paul Hinlicky, a major systematic theologian. He and McDermott published and lectured profusely. We garnered the notice of several ratings agencies as well as the attention of Lutheran donors, who were steered toward endowing more chairs in religion by the church relation's director. The Tise sisters endowed a chair in Lutheran studies and Charles Schumann endowed two chairs—one in theology and one in ethics. That provided four endowed chairs for the religion side of the department.

TEACHING AND WRITING IN THE 80S

Thus, we were slowly able to strengthen the Religion and Philosophy Department, one of Fintel's charges to me. Though we made some gains in that area, I was still somewhat immobilized throughout the 80s by the daunting task of trying to affect the institutional trajectory of the college. But I could go

---

he would become. He also became my closest intellectual friend on the faculty. We met often for lively conversation and planned many events together. His departure after twenty-six years to Beeson Divinity in 2015 was a real loss for me, even though we continue our friendship from afar.

ahead and work on the other tasks before me: teaching theology and ethics, publishing and lecturing beyond the college, and organizing the center. First, teaching. I began teaching four courses per year. The department's offerings included both Christian theology and Christian ethics so I began teaching those. In theology I used Lochmann's *The Faith We Confess: An Ecumenical Dogmatics* and Carl Braaten's *The Principles of Lutheran Theology* and in ethics I used H. R. Niebuhr's *Christ and Culture* and Bonhoeffer's *Ethics*. In the ethics course I used a good deal of the material I had developed at LSTC on the Lutheran teaching on vocation. I found that my students were pretty much unfamiliar with that teaching and I decided that on my first sabbatical I would gather those materials into a book for use by college students and church groups.

When I consented to come to Roanoke College in 1982, I asked that my sabbatical rhythm be honored, which meant that I would have a full year in 1985-86. My family and I returned to Cambridge where I wrote my book on vocation. I was searching for a good title when an imaginative idea popped into my mind. I had just recently seen the movie *Ordinary People* in conjunction with a class on theological interpretation of film that I offered at the college. The main characters in the movie were rich and privileged—extraordinary—on the surface but faced very ordinary challenges at a deeper level. The title was slightly oxymoronic. It occurred to me that Lutherans saw saints as folks who were very ordinary. That is, they were saints before God, not on account of their heroic faith or obedience, but because of the extraordinary grace of God in Christ. Further, as they acted out their discipleship in response to that grace they did so in very ordinary places: in marriage and family life, work, citizenship, and the church. Indeed, they *were* ordinary saints!

That was the main title I proposed to my publisher, Fortress, with the subtitle "An Introduction to the Christian Life." I wanted the text to be broader than just ethics; I wanted it to include the story of salvation and the human place in it, as well as other topics that went beyond ethics. But mainly I wanted it to be a contemporary interpretation of the Lutheran doctrine of vocation. The main question I posed to myself was: what difference does it make to be and act Christianly in the ordinary places in which we live. I argued that the virtues of faith, love, and hope were precisely those qualities that Christians brought to their ordinary responsibilities that transformed them into genuine vocations. They also enabled them to participate critically in each place of responsibility. It made them salt and leaven in the world. I tried to work out how Christian vocation made a difference in marriage and family life, work, citizenship, and church.

The book came out in 1988 and had a number of printings. In 2002 Fortress asked me to write a new revised edition, which then came out in 2003. The book continues to be a key resource in the courses I teach on Christian ethics, in both academic and church contexts. It sells moderately well even after all these years. I dearly hope it has made some contribution to those Christians who strive to lead the Christian life.

Back to teaching at Roanoke College. I also taught courses in theological interpretation of film and capitalism and justice, the latter in which I employed my new book, *The Ethic of Democratic Capitalism: A Moral Reassessment*. I played it off against Philip Wogaman's argument for democratic socialism in his *The Great Economic Debate*. I also taught regularly in the new honors curriculum when it began in the late 80s. I team-taught in both "Formative Visions—Religious and Philosophical Visions that Shaped the West," and "Scientific Milestones and Millstones."

THE CENTER FOR RELIGION AND SOCIETY

Already in the early 80s I had begun serious work on naming and developing the center for which Fintel had raised a significant endowment. Since I was trained in the field of Christian Ethics and Society at the University of Chicago Divinity School, my inclination was to define and develop a center that would foster a lively dialog between Christian intellectual and moral perspectives and the pressing issues of church and society. That seemed to be what Fintel was looking for, so approval of the general thrust came quickly. Here is the definition of the mission of the Roanoke College Center for Church and Society that has persisted for over thirty years:

> The Roanoke College Center for Church[9] and Society aims at bringing to bear Christian religious and moral perspectives—particularly in their Lutheran interpretation—on contemporary challenges to the church and world. Its purpose is to cross boundaries between church and world, sacred and secular, religion and society; to operate at the dynamic interface between religious commitment and the multi-faceted life of the world.

Public lectures that featured speakers of note (especially Lutherans) who would reflect on significant issues facing both church and society. The very first event happened in the spring of 1983 on "Religion and Evolution: Constructive Possibilities," featuring theologian Philip Hefner and biologist Jeffrey Wicken. "The Legacy of Luther" and "Religious Perspectives on National Defense" followed soon thereafter.[10]

The Center proposed and funded interdisciplinary and other needed courses to enrich the College and departmental curriculums. "Religion and Contemporary Literature" was an example of the former and a course in Judaism taught by an observant Orthodox Jew was illustrative of the latter. A pioneering course on the Holocaust was sponsored by the Center.

---

9. In the 90s we substituted "Religion" for "Church" to include Judaism in our offerings.

10. Perhaps the most significant and glamorous event of the Center and the Fowler Program, which provided most of the financial backing, was held in the spring of 1985. The topic of the event was "Germany and the United States: Signals of Danger and Hope," which was examined before several thousand in Bast Gym. It featured Helmut Schmidt, the former Chancellor of West Germany, Walter Stoessel, the US Ambassador to West Germany, Michael Naumann, Senior Foreign Editor of *Der Spiegel*, and Wolfhart Pannenberg, a leading German Lutheran theologian. The lectures

After the "pump was primed" by the Center, the college then took over the funding for these courses when they proved to be important and successful.

Cross-cultural education was enhanced by the Center's proposing and funding travel courses in Africa, Latin America, and Germany.

Continuing education events for clergy and laity were developed, a long-lasting one was Power in the Spirit, a successful summer lay education event at the college jointly sponsored by the Virginia Synod, the Center, and the Roanoke College Office of Church Relations. Other courses in lay theological education were held at the College and in Lutheran churches. Special lectures for clergy on Reformation Day were also featured.

A fruitful partnership between the Center and the Fowler Public Policy Program (under the direction of C. William Hill) emerged in which the Christian and republican traditions of the College were renewed in programs that featured both religious and political perspectives on public issues. This partnership offered fine occasions for faculty, students, and the community to hear high-level discussion of pressing issues. Besides the grand one on the United States and Germany, mentioned in the footnote below, many other collaborations took place. For example, "A Celebration of Liberty—The Constitution, Culture and Change," featuring Martin Marty, James Kilpatrick, and Edward Albee, took place in 1987. Another noteworthy joint program that expressed both the Christian and republican interests of the College took place in 1988 on "The Meaning of Citizenship—Rights and Obli-

---

were later published in book form in an American-German Studies Series sponsored by the University of Virginia: *Germany and the United States: Changing Perceptions/Danger and Hope*, ed. Lore Amlinger, Stuttgart: Academic Publishing House, 1987. A sumptuous reception after Schmidt's evening lecture attended by hundreds was held in a newly-opened Marriott Hotel in Roanoke that featured food prepared by a German chef brought in from Washington DC.

gations in the 1990s" and featured Robert Bellah, Lawrence Mead, and William Raspberry. For several years we offered panel discussions of current events on the local public television and radio stations.

Scores of lectures followed in the ensuing years. The most stellar event ever sponsored solely by the Center happened in the spring of 2007, when famed New Testament scholar and Bishop N.T. Wright of England lectured on "The Resurrection of the Son of God" to a crowd of nearly three thousand who packed Bast Gym on a Friday evening amid much competition for the public's attention. Bishop Wright also spoke at other venues at the college as well as at churches in the Roanoke Valley. It was highly unusual for someone of that "star power" to stay as a guest of the Center over an extended weekend. The Bishop made a great impact.

Closely following the bishop in importance was the last public lecture of Richard John Neuhaus before he died of cancer in January of 2010. Neuhaus, whom I had known for many years, came to the college to lecture on "Moral Imperatives and Political Choices: A Christian Response" in October of 2008, right before the election of Barack Obama. I expected that he would be very feisty and partisan since he was intensely committed to the pro-life cause, which would be weakened by an Obama presidency. However, he avoided any directly partisan remarks and rather plumbed deep Christian themes that he thought Christians of all political stripes should pursue. After the lecture, a small group of his friends gathered around him at our home for conversation. Rather than his usual effusive self, Richard was mellow and pensive. When I took him to the airport I had the melancholy thought that this would be our last meeting. It was.

Another initiative of the Center was the establishment of a series of Faith and Reason gatherings that commenced in 2003 and continues to the present day. In these gatherings faculty and top-level administrators—including the President—are asked to reflect on how their faith impacts their work at the College—teaching, research, treatment of students, administrative work. There are no constraints on what "faith" means or on what, if any, are the effects of their faith on their work. Manuscripts of the talks are requested; honoraria are bestowed. The lectures, held three or four times an academic year, are followed by a fine dinner in the President's Dining Room of the College's Colket Student Center. Over dessert the assembled audience—running from 20-30—carries on a lively conversation in response to the lecture. This series provides the opportunity and challenge for faculty to relate their religious convictions to their intellectual life on campus. Over the years about a third of the faculty have contributed or attended at one time or another.

About the same time another program of the Center emerged: the annual Crumley Lecture. James Crumley was a 1948 graduate of Roanoke College who went on to a long and distinguished career in the Lutheran Church in America, culminating in his becoming the President (and then Presiding Bishop) of that church from 1978 to 1987. His friends gave a considerable gift to the College in his honor that provided an endowment for an annual lecture, which began in 1999 and continues to the present time. The lecture is given by an outstanding Lutheran lay person who reflects on how his faith is expressed in his vocation. It has featured business executives, scientists, journalists, professors, judges, artists, and choral directors, among others. It draws an audience of distinguished lay persons from the featured professions as well as an array of Virginia Lutherans for the lecture and a celebrative dinner at which a report on the activities of the Center is given. In later years the lecture has been widened to include non-Lutheran lecturers and opened to a wider audience of students and members of the community that often fills the four hundred seats of Olin Theater.

Yet another initiative of the Center was the establishment of the Blakely Evangelical Studies program. Thomas Blakely was a prominent Salem citizen and Baptist churchman who bequeathed an endowment for the program. Since Gerald McDermott owned evangelical credentials the program came under his direction. He used its resources to invite many evangelical speakers to campus as well as to support his lecture trips to many countries around the world—including Cuba, Hungary, Poland, and Slovakia.

A final new launch for the Center was its Slovak program. Directed by Paul Hinlicky, newly arrived in 1999 from his teaching stint in Slovakia, the program enabled Slovak students to come to Roanoke College to study and newly-minted Slovak Ph.D.s to teach at the College. It also supported the efforts of several Roanoke College professors to teach at the Lutheran theological faculty of the Comenius University in Bratislava. I had the opportunity to teach Christian ethics twice at that seminary. Besides the teaching, the two stints were wonderful occasions to drink in the culture and beauty of Bratislava, the capitol of Slovakia. In addition, the Center published two books on religion and society in Slovakia edited by one of those newly-minted Ph.D.s.

THE SCHOLARLY REPUTATION OF THE COLLEGE

In the 80s, then, we were able to strengthen the Religion and Philosophy Department and to define and organize the Center for Religion and Society, both of which strengthened the college's relation to its Lutheran heritage. Another purpose Fintel had in hiring me was to help lift the scholarly reputation of the college. Though the college included many good teachers, few published or lectured outside the college in the early 80s. Actually, something of a tradition of pride in non-publishing had evolved over the years. The faculty—except for one or two—were proud to be part of a college devoted solely to teaching.

The first several years after my arrival I published and lectured far more than anyone else. But the arrival of Dean

Gerald Gibson changed the ethos of the college. He was intent on encouraging the ongoing scholarly activity of faculty. In order to honor those who were involved in scholarly writing and lecturing, he instituted a publication that listed those activities by the faculty. At the beginning its issues were rather slim but soon began to expand, partly because of his insistence that faculty continue scholarly lives, but also because the new faculty coming out of the graduate schools in the mid- to later-80s were intent on continuing scholarly pursuits. In compensation for this new emphasis on publishing and external lecturing, Gibson was able to reduce the teaching load for many faculty. His insistence on ongoing scholarly activity by the faculty was met with anger by some of the older guard who wanted the college to be devoted strictly to teaching. They organized a no-confidence petition that was sent to the new president, David Gring, in 1989. They didn't succeed in getting rid of Gibson but they did undermine his influence in academic affairs. However, he appreciated and encouraged my efforts.

To stimulate scholarly activity I initiated two further activities. One was to invite faculty from other departments to appear at a seminar sponsored by our department to report formally on their research activities. Another was to run "Front Burner" noon gatherings at which faculty were invited to talk informally about what was foremost in their scholarly interests and productions. I asked department chairs which faculty were doing interesting research in their departments and they then pointed me to candidates, whom I then asked to report. The secret of the success of those sessions was their informality. We met at noon in a room around a large table without any provision for lunch. Some faculty brought their own, some went through the cafeteria line, some didn't lunch. And it made no difference to me how many faculty showed up. The presenter told what was making him or her tick, and we had fine discussions.

By now I had made some progress on three of the four fronts that Fintel had put forward to me: strengthening the Religion and Philosophy Department, defining and organizing a center, and helping to lift the scholarly activity and reputation of the college. Of course I did not do these things alone; I was part of a larger movement. But things were moving in the right direction.

THE IDENTITY AND MISSION OF THE COLLEGE

How about the overall identity and mission of the college? I was still puzzled about how and why the college had secularized so extensively. I had read the fine history of the college up until 1942 by William Eisenberg entitled *The First Hundred Years: Roanoke College*. The author simply assumed that the college was deeply Christian and told charming stories of key people and events in the college's history. He did little critical interpretation of that history over one hundred years.

Two later histories of the college offered only tangential reflection on its changing identity and mission. I still wondered what had slowly re-fashioned the college. How did the public relevance of its Christian heritage get so diminished?

Beginning in the early 90s, a first step in answering that question involved an ongoing conversation among interested faculty and administrators about the nature and mission of a church-related college. These "faith and learning" meetings were held three times each term over breakfast. Ten to fifteen faculty and administrators attended regularly. The conversations centered on the burgeoning literature on the plight and promise of Christian higher education. Foremost among them were articles by James Burtchaell published in *First Things* in the early 90s entitled "The Rise and Fall of the Christian College," which traced the trajectory of Vanderbilt University from its founders early vision of it as the Protestant equivalent of Notre Dame to its complete secularization. Burtchaell followed these up in 1998 with a huge study of the secularization processes in seventeen colleges and universities. He boldly entitled the book *The Dying of the Light: The Disengagement of Colleges and Universities from their Christian Churches* (Eerdmans, 1998). The topic of the ongoing Roanoke conversation was: is this happening here? If so, what can we do to retard or reverse it?

These conversations issued in at least two initiatives that were supported by President Gring, who succeeded Fintel in 1989. Both were important in strengthening the Christian heritage of the College. The first was membership in the Lilly Network of Church-Related Colleges and Universities, which entailed a significant membership fee. The College was an early joiner in 1996. The Network holds conferences attended by representatives of its member schools that probe the challenges of Christian higher education. Representatives from Roanoke attend each year and bring back constructive ideas about how it might increase commitment to the religious element in its mission.

A major curricular development of the 90s deserves mention. A new general education curriculum finally replaced the incoherent "distribution" curriculum that had reigned at Roanoke since the late 60s. The new curriculum featured the return of a required religion/philosophy course after many years of religion courses being merely a choice among many others in the specified area of the humanities. The new curriculum built on an honors curriculum that had been constructed for a new honors program in the mid-80s under the encouragement of Dean Gibson. I was involved in the development of that earlier honors curriculum, which featured many interdisciplinary courses and a capstone course in which students were required to marshal their learnings by applying them to a contemporary challenge in society. Drawing on the work of Richard McKeon, which I had encountered at the University of Chicago, I argued that every discipline has certain fundamental assumptions and methods that could be examined in the interdisciplinary courses. "Formative Visions" was a first year theology and philosophy course that examined the key visions of meaning and values that shaped the life of the West. Other courses were "Wealth and Power," "The Artistic Imagination," "Scientific Millstones and Milestones," and "Turning Points in History." It presented a coherent curriculum to excellent students.

Patterned to some extent after that honors curriculum, the new general education program of studies was planned in the late 80s and initiated in the early 90s. It lasted for over 20 years. It, too, was fairly coherent and involved a junior level course entitled "Values and the Responsible Life," that I had designed. The earlier honors curriculum was relatively easy to get through the faculty because only a portion of the professors and student body were involved in it. Getting this one through the faculty was another matter. Strong sentiment was expressed against a required religion course, but the "values" course was attractive enough to the whole faculty that it passed, along with the rest of the curriculum. In that course we offered a good deal of Western ethical philosophy and moral theology with a smattering of the world religions. The whole point was to get students to think seriously about their own values and how they might be grounded in and enriched by the great philosophical and religious traditions of the West. In my version of the course I took up the Lutheran teaching on vocation as a way to consider the responsible life. At the end of the course the students were required to take up "contemporary challenges" in the light of their learnings.

Both curricula involved required religion courses that indicated that the college thought student engagement with the Christian heritage was important. We seemed to be making modest progress in making that heritage publicly relevant again, especially in the college's curriculum. Yet, we found that it—the values course in the general education curriculum—was the most monitored course in the curriculum by the general education director. She was suspicious that we were proselytizing the students, and made sure that non-Christian perspectives were offered. Meanwhile, of course, feminists were heavy-handed in their efforts to make sure that all courses included feminist perspectives and that the language used was sufficiently "non-sexist." No monitoring was required of those courses.

FURTHER WRITINGS

In 1992 Mark Noll, the distinguished evangelical historian, wrote an article entitled "The Lutheran Difference" in an issue of *First Things*. In it he called for a stronger voice in American religion and public life for a Lutheran interpretation of the relation of religion and politics, one that could challenge the ascendant one in American history. That history, he argued, had been shaped by the Reformed tradition, which applied a strong notion of personal sanctification to the public, political sphere. It tended to claim that political programs, shaped by vigorous religion, could become approximations of the kingdom of God. That, he thought, claimed too much for politics. At its worst it bred messianic politics and politicized religion. He knew that Lutheranism bore a different conception of the relation of religion and politics and called for it to provide an alternative—Pauline, Augustinian, and Lutheran.

His call was right what I needed to take up that cause. Besides, I wanted to supplement my *Ordinary Saints*, which focused on individual vocations, with an argument about the church's vocation in the political sphere. So in 1992 we again went to Cambridge, England, where I wrote *The Paradoxical Vision—A Public Theology for the 21st Century*. In that book, which was published by Fortress in 1995, I did just what Noll called for. I surveyed the sorts of public theologies extant in America and then argued for a Lutheran point of view, sometimes called the "two kingdoms" approach. Actually, it is better to talk of the "two ways that God reigns in the world" in order to avoid spatializing God's presence and action.

This "two-ways" thinking makes a distinction—but not a separation—between the work of God's left hand, his law, and of his right hand, the Gospel. The law encompasses all those mysterious works of God that create, judge, limit, and sustain the world through many agencies. They keep a basic order and a modicum of justice in the face of all those forces that wreak chaos and injustice. One of those agencies is politics, but of a definitely non-redemptive sort. Whatever we do politically through human action does not bring salvation; it brings order and justice of a distinctly limited sort. This does not mean there is no progress in history, but neither does it mean that progress is certain. There can be regress and disaster. So we can rejoice in a stable world that also retains the possibility of an enhanced justice. We should work with the God's law for a better world. But we should not look for salvation there. Thus, Lutherans could never call America the "redeemer nation."

The work of the Gospel is quite another matter. In that realm, Christians are totally receptive. They receive the Gospel of God's grace in Christ through the power of the Holy Spirit which opens their hearts to that grace. They receive it with gratitude and rejoicing, for faith in the Gospel insures the Christian's eternal destiny. We become saints before God not because of our heroic deeds or faith, but because of the extravagant grace of God offered to us in Christ. Then, however, as we receive that grace we respond by becoming servants of our neighbor in our various callings. We become conduits of God's love. It is the church's great mission to be the instrument of God's right hand, to proclaim salvation by grace through faith on account of Christ.

I followed this basic Lutheran distinction by showing the dangers of confusing the law with the Gospel and vice-versa, in the first case mistaking our actions as redemptive and in the second case applying the radical ethic of the Gospel directly to political life.

In the final section of the book I showed how the church then influences society, both indirectly and directly. I argue that the church should prefer the indirect approach through its well-formed laity and voluntary associations, which then avoids the temptation of the church to become too identified with a political ideology or party. The more direct ways—social statements or pronouncements and direct involvement in political action—should be used sparingly because they do run the risk of religion becoming politicized and politics becoming religionized. Both distortions then diminish the transcendent message of the church. There have been far too many instances in history that illustrate this danger. Even in America there is such a temptation.

The book received good reviews in some prestigious journals—*First Things* being one—and it continues to sell modestly. But it certainly did not change the general direction of religious involvement in politics in America. Evangelicals have tended to identify too closely with conservative politics and liberal Protestants too closely with liberal parties and causes. The "Lutheran difference" did not take hold, though in more recent years evangelical leaders have grown more reluctant to identify too closely with conservative politics. I wish I could say the same about mainline Protestantism. But the Lutheran Church—Missouri Synod and the new North American Lutheran Church heeded—or perhaps they already agreed with—what I argued in *The Paradoxical Vision*. The LCMS Statement on Church-State relations quoted it amply and the NALC, in which I have had some influence, has avoided the kind of direct modes of action that liberal Protestants too often adopt.

During that same sabbatical year I took up another book-writing project that provided light relief from the heavy task of writing on public theology. In the mornings I would write on public theology while in the afternoons I would turn to writing a small book on my approach to interpreting film. I had been offering a course on film interpretation for many years in which I drew upon the narrative analysis of great literature by Preston Roberts, a professor I had at the University of Chicago Divinity School way back in the early 60s. I combined that approach with the kind of analysis done in the Ecumenical

Institute's Religious Studies I. (See more about both the course and the Institute above.) I developed it so that the serious dramatic movies we examined in the course could be identified as Christian (explicit and implicit), American Dream, Greek Tragic, or Skeptical. I conveyed my interpretative approach in lectures and courses while I sought for a book that could do in print what I was doing orally. To no avail.

The courses on movie interpretation were highly successful when I offered them. I began each course by promising the students that they would never view serious movies the same after they took the course. Many enthusiastically agreed by its end. Few courses that I have offered have had such a clear effect on those who have taken them. Since the approach was so successful I thought it was time to write it up in a book, which I did during that year in Cambridge. I named it *Seeing is Believing: Visions of Life in Film*. After I finished it I tried unsuccessfully to get major companies to publish it. But the University Press of America, which published academic books that didn't appear to be profitable to major companies, took me up and published it in 1998. While never selling large numbers, it is still in print and I use it in the courses I teach on film interpretation until the present day.

While having little effect on the world of secular movie interpretation, my approach at least assumes that serious movies have real meaning, both philosophical and theological. That's what students seem to appreciate about the course.

TAKING UP THE CAUSE OF CHRISTIAN HIGHER EDUCATION

By the late 90s I had reflected a good deal on the plight and destiny of Christian higher education. I had been stimulated by the "faith and learning" conversations that had earlier gone on among faculty and administrators who were sympathetic to preserving the Christian heritage of the college. In those sessions we had been reading and discussing the expanding literature on Christian higher education, especially those books and articles that documented its secularization. Prime among them was Burtchaell's magnificent but pessimistic book—*The Dying of the Light: the Disengagement of Colleges and Universities from the Christian Churches*.

I was now ready to make my own contribution to the larger discussion and apply it to the Roanoke situation. I applied for the Senior Fellow position at the Lilly Fellows Program in Humanities and the Arts at Valparaiso University for my last sabbatical year, 1999-2000. I won the competition and my wife and I moved to Valparaiso, Indiana, for the year. This was our first sabbatical without children in tow. The Lilly program was ideal for the research project I had in mind. It involved six Lilly Fellows who had just earned their Ph. D.s and were teaching at Valparaiso in anticipation of their being hired by one of the church-related colleges or universities of the far-flung Lilly Network of Church-Related Colleges. They were intensely interested in Christian higher education. I had a weekly seminar with the young Fellows in which I presented my unfolding work for their perusal and response. Further, the university had many administrators and faculty who were committed to robust Christian higher education and who were interested in my work. They offered friendly advice and criticism as my work progressed.

I organized my project in response to Burtchaell's pessimistic outlook. I was sure there were excellent colleges and universities who had "kept the faith" or "preserved the light" and that those schools were not of a uniform sort. I fully accepted Burtchaell's account of the schools he examined, but thought there were exceptions to his dismal view and that such schools were "Christian" in various degrees, not in the "wholly-or-not-at-all" assessment he preferred.

My first step was to select colleges and universities that I thought were faithful to their sponsoring religious traditions.

Further, I wanted to examine colleges that were considered to be excellent by various rating agencies. I didn't want my examples of faithfulness to be weak academic institutions so that critics could charge that "religious" schools are inevitably weak academically.

I had enough general knowledge to wager that Wheaton among the evangelical schools and Calvin among the Christian Reformed schools "kept the faith" in very significant ways. They were also well-regarded academically. I knew that both Valparaiso University and St. Olaf College were at that time serious about their Lutheran heritages and were academically excellent. Besides, I was resident in one of them. The other, St. Olaf, had been given high marks in the "faithfulness" category even by Burtchaell, who, at the very end of a positive assessment, cryptically remarked that its fidelity to the Lutheran tradition would be gone within a generation.

I wanted to move beyond the liberal arts category to larger research universities in my study, particularly since it was a truism that universities left their religious identities behind as they rose to research status. A likely candidate to disprove that thesis was Notre Dame, which was conveniently right down the road from Valparaiso in South Bend. So Notre Dame was my first candidate; my second was Baylor University. I had read about the controversial attempts at Baylor to strengthen its Christian identity as it rose in the rankings of research universities. Besides, one of the leaders of those Baylor efforts, Provost Don Schmeltekopf, had heard about my research and invited me to address the presidents and provosts of a number of Baptist schools at O'Hare airport in Chicago in the fall of 1999. He invited me to visit Baylor after I indicated that I was interested in what was happening there.

So I had my candidates. Before I visited the colleges I reviewed the vast literature on the secularization of church-related schools and summarized the secularizing forces at work in all church-related colleges and universities. I wanted to be clear about what those schools were facing. After all, the narrative of de-Christianization was far more dominant than of "keeping the faith."

Then I studied the catalogues and rhetoric of each school I was to visit. I tried as best I could to get an accurate and comprehensive portrait of each school and how they did or did not maintain their "soul." From that study I determined that one could discern how schools could "keep their soul" under three basic rubrics: the theological vision that guided the school in all its facets; the ethos or "way of life" that was expressed in the school's practices that shaped its character; and the people who embraced the vision and embodied the ethos of school. I was particularly interested in how much "faith-learning" engagement was going on in each of the schools, i.e., to what extent faculty engaged their Christian intellectual and moral convictions with their secular fields of learning. Those factors became the keys by which I analyzed each school I set out to visit.

I also developed a typology of Christian schools based upon my reading of the six, all of which I thought were "robust" Christian schools in which the theological vision and religious ethos were paradigmatic for the life of the school. Each school hired for mission: they selected people who knew the vision and embodied the ethos. The robust schools divided into two categories: the "orthodox" and the "critical mass." The first insisted that everyone—administrators, faculty, staff—be members of a particular religious tradition. Both Wheaton (evangelical) and Calvin (Reformed) illustrated that sub-type. The critical mass schools—Baylor, Notre Dame, St. Olaf, Valparaiso—all tried to recruit a "critical mass" of members of its sponsoring religious tradition among its administrators, faculty, staff, and students. Those two types, I thought, "kept the soul" publicly relevant in every facet of the life of the school.

When schools no longer insisted that a theological vision guide the life of the school but yet wanted to claim continuing status as "church-related" or "Christian" schools, I developed another category—a third type— which I called "intentional pluralist." Such schools guaranteed a "place at the table" for those who carried the vision and ethos of the sponsoring religious tradition, but did not privilege them beyond that. I thought many church-related colleges—including Roanoke—fit that category well. The fourth and last type was what I called "accidental pluralist." In such schools the sponsoring tradition was presently there by accident, not intention. Those types of schools were essentially secular though they often wanted to keep the historic religious connection visible in some way—an old chapel, a chaplain, some scholarships, and perhaps even a motto. Their sponsoring religious tradition was publicly irrelevant except for those tidbits.

With that extensive preparation, I arranged roughly weeklong visits to each school. During that time I tried to speak with each major constituency of the school, including board members. It was an exciting experience because I learned first-hand how each school "kept the faith" or effectively combined "quality with soul." Essentially, it came down to having a robust theological vision for the school that was taken seriously in hiring and in cultivating practices that embodied the vision. For that you needed people who unabashedly knew and expressed the tradition.

Eerdmans, which had a history of publishing work on Christian higher education (they published Burtchaell's tome), showed real interest and we signed a contract. Interestingly, the editor assigned to me later became the head editor of the company. When I sent the finished manuscript to Eerdmans I proposed the title: *Quality with Soul: How Six Premier Colleges and Universities Keep Faith with Their Religious Traditions*. Several editors did not think the word "soul" conveyed what I wanted it to, but I thought it did. "Soul" certainly conveys the religious element in a school's identity, but it also carries a bit more: what combines with that religious element to give particular character to the school. St. Olaf is not only Lutheran but also a school with a fantastic choral music tradition. Notre Dame is not only Catholic but also a symbol of Catholic fighting spirit in athletics. After a bit of a tussle, I won the argument and that became its title. I liked "soul" enough to use it for another book that I wrote much later, to which I will refer later.

The book came out in 2001 soon after I returned from my sabbatical. It received a number of positive reviews, but, more importantly, it landed me many speaking and consulting opportunities over the years, right up until the present day. I have worked with Baptist, Methodist, Mennonite, Seventh Day Adventist, Lutheran, Church of God, Church of Christ, Wesleyan, Swedenborgian, Catholic, and other schools. Perhaps the most important role was that of presenter for almost a decade in Baylor's Leadership Seminar, a yearly summer event organized by former Provost Don Schmeltekopf, which trained many leaders of Southern Baptist colleges and universities, including the current president of Baylor. Recent books on Christian higher education even refer to the "classic Benne typology." *Quality with Soul* has sold over ten thousand volumes and continues to sell fairly well. I think it has had the most practical or institutional effect of anything I have written. I am delighted that it has helped schools "keep their souls."

After the book came out I waited with anxious anticipation for the review that would likely come from James Burtchaell, the high prophet of secularization. I knew him personally and was quite aware that he did not suffer fools gladly. I feared that he would think I was way too optimistic about the schools I examined. I was surprised—and relieved—to find out that he had been interdicted by his religious order for his sharp attacks on a number of Catholic schools he had analyzed in his *Dying of the Light*. Since he was prohibited from writing publicly about Christian higher education, I did not need to fear public rebuke. However, about a year after my book's appearance a fat envelop appeared in my mailbox with Burtchaell's return address. Though apprehensive, I was delighted that he complimented me graciously about the analysis I had done, but ended with the verdict: only the "orthodox" schools would persist as robust Christian schools into the future. What I called "critical mass" and "intentionally pluralist" schools he deemed "unstable," and likely to succumb to secularization over the long run. That judgment helped make sense of the cryptic verdict at the end of his mostly laudatory appraisal of St. Olaf in the *Dying of the Light* that its "soul" would disappear in a generation. Though I thought his appraisal of the future of those schools too dark, I have come to believe Burtchaell was more right than wrong. I am reminded of Richard John Neuhaus' "law:" "When orthodoxy becomes optional it eventually becomes proscribed." Much more on this later.

Before I took my sabbatical in 1999-2000 I told President Gring that I wanted to leave my tenured position on the faculty after my sabbatical. I had become weary trying to do too many things: teach four courses, chair the department, run the Center with all its programs, preside over the "Front Burner" gatherings, and carry on a rather heavy schedule of lecturing and writing. I should have just given up some of those roles but I didn't. Further, I had just arranged for Paul Hinlicky to come from his teaching position in Slovakia to occupy the Jordan-Trexler Chair of Religion, which I would be vacating. I told Gring I would like to continue to direct the Center for Religion and Society and teach a course here and there as an adjunct. He kindly asked me to think about such a drastic decision at age 63. I did think about it but decided to take leave of my faculty position. I would get rid of a lot of things I found burdensome but keep those things that I enjoyed and thought were useful to the college and church.

While I was on that sabbatical an interesting step forward was taken by the faculty. The college had not updated its statement of purpose for many years and its accrediting agency insisted that it do so. This was an opportunity to strengthen the college's relation to its Lutheran heritage by articulating something beyond its weak earlier statement that it would "honor its Lutheran heritage while welcoming those of all faiths."

The new statement expanded both the moral and religious elements in its purposes. The college's classic republican tradition—supplying virtuous students from all walks of life for service to the community, country, and world—is noticeably present. Its religious tradition—the Christian tradition broadly defined—is also visible. "Spiritual growth," "engaging in moral and social issues," "participating in religious life," "honoring its Christian heritage and partnership with the Lutheran church," and especially "nurturing a dialogue between faith and reason" were stronger signals of the college's religious heritage than those in the earlier statement, which had been written in the late 1960s. A good deal of this advance could be attributed to the work of the "faith and learning" group that had met throughout the 1990s. It was also aided by a faculty workshop—including administrators and Board members—on "Honoring Our Christian Heritage" that I organized in 1995 featuring Martin Marty, the distinguished church historian of the University of Chicago.

While there were skirmishes about many planks in the College's new platform—some faculty preferred "spiritual" rather than "religious"—it was the commitment to "nurturing a dialogue between faith and reason" that really provoked a battle when it was proposed. The phrase, of course, came right out of the extended discussion in the "faith and learning group" of the necessity of a church-related college to foster just such a dialogue. After heated discussion, the faculty voted exactly evenly. The moderator of the faculty, a devout Catholic, broke the tie. Uneasy with such a result, she brought the issue up again for another vote at the next faculty meeting. This time the new provision passed handily. This was an enormous gain for those who wanted the College to strengthen its relation to its Christian heritage, especially to its intellectual dimension. But the conflict in the faculty over this new plank was a harbinger of the strife to come, to which we will now turn.

A PAINFUL DEFEAT

Right after I returned to the college in the summer of 2000 the Lilly Endowment offered an exciting opportunity for colleges and universities who were church-related in some way. Lilly made 20 two million dollar grants available to schools that would make "vocation" a central theme of their college life. The Lilly Endowment has a huge section devoted to religious affairs and this program was meant to help many secularizing schools regain some religious substance by making a key Christian (especially Lutheran) teaching a publicly relevant concept for their faculty and students. Lilly would not simply give these grants away, but would award them in a competitive process.

What an exciting prospect! If Roanoke College won such a grant we could perhaps articulate and realize a clearer sense of identity and mission. We could draw the college closer to its Christian heritage. It was especially inviting because as a Lutheran-related school we already had some acquaintance with the Lutheran teaching on vocation. Several of us had repeatedly taught the Lutheran doctrine of vocation in the required religion/philosophy course. All we needed to do was to find a way to organize our curricular and non-curricular offerings around that lively teaching. Moreover, such a focus would be consistent with the historic Roanoke commitment to Christian service to church and society. It seemed to be a no-brainer.

Since I had just returned from a year with the Lilly Fellows Program at Valparaiso and had just written a book on Christian higher education I was a natural candidate to lead the Roanoke College effort to get a planning grant and then apply for the two-million dollar bonanza. Besides, I was no longer officially a full-time faculty member. President Gring asked me to lead the task force that would spearhead the effort to get a planning grant and then the full award. I eagerly accepted the invitation because I thought it was a perfect time to fulfill that charge made to me long ago by President Fintel: to bring the college closer to its Lutheran/Christian heritage. It seemed providential that this opportunity came up at just the right moment for me and the college.

I wrote a proposal for the planning grant in late 2000 that was accepted by the Lilly office. A Lilly Grant Planning

Committee was then organized. It included the President, the Chaplain, the Director of Church Relations, the Chair of the Religion and Philosophy Department, four faculty who had been involved in programs of the Center for Religion and Society, a Board member, and several students.

The group worked hard for the months following the acquisition of the planning grant. It came up with a robust proposal that was offered to the faculty in a meeting in August of 2001, right before the September 11 attacks. The heart of the proposal put vocation in the center of the required curriculum, organizing departmental offerings to enable students to discern and prepare for their callings in their work and citizenship, but also in marriage and family life, and the church. It did not insist that students adhere to a fully Christian notion of vocation but it did give substantial direction toward living a purposeful life.

On the morning of the faculty meeting, members of the planning committee gave reports to flesh out the recommendations of the proposal, which involved curricular change, and then opened the meeting to discussion. A concerted, relentless attack on the proposal then followed for the rest of the morning. It was the longest morning of my life. The secularist wing of the faculty, led by a group of openly secularist department chairs, had done their homework and carefully planned the assault.

The opponents dredged up an article I had written in *The Christian Century* in the spring of 2001 entitled "Reconnecting a College with its Christian Heritage" in which I recounted the gains we had made in the 1980s and 1990s in strengthening the Christian element in the College's identity and mission, much the way I have listed these gains in this chapter. One of the hostile leaders copied the article and distributed it to a network that was intent on torpedoing the proposal. Toward the end of the article I mentioned that the College was attempting to get a Lilly grant to make vocation an organizing principle in the life the College. I brashly predicted that we would get the grant and that it would enable the proposed program to "be implemented across the curriculum." That overly confident statement was brought to the attention of the faculty and scathingly criticized as presumptuous and dangerous, a threat to faculty freedom. Other arguments were marshalled, too, one against the proposal to recruit more Lutheran students. One of the secularist department chairs contemptuously allowed that those "dear little Lutherans angels will no doubt make great contributions in our classes."

Beyond the members of the committee, few spoke in favor of the proposal. Many faculty were aghast at the vigor of the resistance. Junior faculty who might have been supportive were often in departments chaired by vehement opponents and were intimidated. The non-committed middle of the faculty tended to side with the opponents because they wanted things to stay as they were. That's when I found out that those who thought the college's relation to its Christian heritage was "just right" would vigorously resist any strengthening of that connection. Any forward movement was likely to be oppressive in their minds. Though no vote was taken, none had to. The secularists clearly held sway.

This episode resulted in many painful hours of reflection on my part. At first I was angry with President Gring for not supporting the original proposal in spite of the protest. But perhaps he foresaw too much conflict down the road when the College would try to implement the central proposals. Perhaps it was wiser to risk losing the grant than to invite open conflict and opposition by the faculty. For my part, I saw many mistakes in hindsight. The first grand error can be attributed to hybris: I thought we had triumphed over the secularists and they were in retreat. Hadn't we just engineered a stronger statement of purpose? Hadn't we gathered more and more faculty in the "faith and learning" group? Didn't we have the president firmly on our side? Sadly, though, I underestimated the strength and resolve of the secularist wing while I overestimated the effects of what we had done in the 1980s and 1990s to advance the Christian cause. I should have noted that the split in the faculty over the clause in the new Statement of Purpose that talked of "nurturing a dialogue between faith and reason" was a sign that we had not "won" over the secularists. In my complacence I had not organized support from the general faculty for the proposal. The second mistake was that our proposal had many curricular implications that frightened and angered the faculty. When I studied the successful proposals of those colleges that later won grants, I noticed that few had proposed curricular changes for their colleges but rather located most of the Lilly initiatives in the non-curricular areas of college life. Faculties are notoriously jealous of their control over curricula and I should have anticipated that. Finally, I should have insisted that President Gring assess the final proposal more intensely. He was a man of conservative temper and he might have detected the mistakes that were made had I insisted that he pay closer attention to the proposal.

Many years later when I was writing my book on the history of Roanoke College, Gring told me he was shocked by this "unfortunate eruption of anti-religious paranoia." Yet, at the time of the conflict he decided that the dissenters had to be taken seriously. He assigned the new interim Dean of the Faculty the job of revising the proposal after meeting with the dissenters. The final proposal sent to the Lilly Foundation was very different from the first. Many bold proposals were revised or eliminated. Qualifiers were attached. The selection committee of the Lilly initiative found the proposal to be "ambivalent," and turned it down. When news of Lilly's rejection of the proposal became known, a celebration took place by the "winners."

The hope to move Christian vocation to a central organizing principle of the College was dashed.

PICKING UP THE PIECES

While the faculty defeated our proposal—and thereby lost a two million dollar grant for the college, life went on. The president who in 2004 followed Gring, Sabine O'Hara, actually had the capacity and the interest to be bolder in giving Christian substance to the college mission. She appointed a task force to write a "principles and philosophy" addendum to the college purpose statement. But the addendum remained consistently formal in its articulation of the college's self-understanding. It could not bring itself to use any Christian principles or rhetoric as a basis of the college commitment to service. O'Hara departed in 2007 before she could insist on Lutheran substance.

That did not mean that all was lost. In the first decade of the 21st century the Religion and Philosophy Department was significantly strengthened by the addition of three more endowed chairs. The church relations director, Kathryn Buchanan, along with the presidents and I approached wealthy Lutheran donors to endow those chairs. Three Tise sisters honored their pastor father by endowing the Tise Chair in Lutheran Studies, which was soon occupied by Paul Hinlicky. Charles and Helen Schumann endowed two more chairs, one in Lutheran theology that was offered to Ned Wisnefske, and one in Christian ethics, which was offered to James Peterson, who succeeded me as the department's Christian ethicist and as the college's Director of the Center for Religion and Society. Happily, the Center was named after me when I handed over the directorship of the center to Peterson in the spring of 2012. The Jordan-Trexler Professor of Religion chair was vacated by Hinlicky and offered to Gerald McDermott. The professors who occupied the endowed chairs became amazingly productive in the years between 2000 and 2015. Scores of books were published and countless lectures here and abroad were given, especially by McDermott and Hinlicky. Peterson also added to the total, as did I with my continued writing and lecturing. That period was a golden age of intellectual production by the religion faculty of the department. No other department came close to that level of scholarly achievement. I am proud to have had a role in building it.

Though I was no longer on the faculty of the college, I continued to write short pieces for *First Things*, *The Roanoke*

Times, Lutheran Forum, Forum Letter, Juicy Ecumenism, Lutheran Quarterly, The Philadelphia Inquirer, and *RealClearReligion.* More seriously, I was able to get a book on religion and politics published in 2010 by Eerdmans entitled *Good and Bad Ways to Think about Religion and Politics.* Annoyed by the many public misconceptions about the relation of religion and politics in America—especially the tendency to confuse the separation of church and state with the interaction of religion and politics, I launched out on what I thought was a far more accurate and persuasive way of relating the two. I started the book with chapters on two bad ways to relate religion and politics: separationism and fusion. Then I launched into my own view, which I called "critical engagement." I argue that core Christian teachings do in fact engage political ideologies and policies, but generally in indirect ways. There are many other factors that work their way into Christian political judgments and actions, making it rare that there are "Christian" policies or ideologies. But core Christian convictions are definitely in the mix, and, sometimes are the dominating factor. I show how religious beliefs and movements have affected American political life dramatically, and how such efforts are constitutionally, historically, and theologically proper. I finish the book with my well-worn typology of how organized religion does and should affect political life. I argue for a strong preference for indirect ways of religious involvement in politics: through the laity and through voluntary associations, but do allow for singular cases in which the church must both speak and act directly as a religious body.

The book received excellent reviews in *First Things* and *The Weekly Standard*, and has garnered me numerous speaking engagements, though it did not have the wider influence I thought it deserved.

Also in 2010, a Lutheran pastor, friend, and avid reader of my writings, Michael Shahan, organized and edited a Festschrift (a celebrative volume honoring me on my 70th birthday) that was published by Eerdmans. Entitled *Report from the Front Lines:*

Conversations on Public Theology, it contains chapters by such well-known authors and friends: Carl Braaten, John Stumme, Richard Neuhaus, Jean Bethke Elshtain, Mark Noll, Gilbert Meilaender, Paul Hinlicky, Gerald McDermott, Ronald Thiemann, and Donald Schmeltekopf, among others. When the volume was published, McDermott organized a public celebration in the college chapel featuring Carl Braaten.

A few years earlier, I was asked by an editor at Concordia Publishing House to compile my many occasional writings into a book to be published by that press. I had written so many editorials, columns, and chapters in books that I was delighted to grasp the opportunity. I gathered what I thought would be most interesting and organized the pieces into an orderly presentation. Concordia named it *Reasonable Ethics: A Christian Approach to Social, Economic, and Political Concerns*. I was not too keen on the title, which seemed to be both pretentious and unclear at the same time. It has sold modestly and is still in print. I am happy that some of my favorite short pieces have been preserved in book form.

In the same period I was asked to join the board of the American Lutheran Publicity Bureau, a pan-Lutheran organization that represents and encourages an "evangelical catholic" expression of Lutheranism. I discussed this tradition earlier in the chapter on the church. It has been a happy experience to work with an organization that is deeply Lutheran, orthodox, liturgical, and catholic in the best sense of the word. The organization's most significant accomplishment in recent decades has been the compiling and publishing of a four volume breviary, *For All the Saints: A Prayer Book by and for the Church*. It has also published many books relevant to Lutheranism that would not be published by the mainstream press. In 2014 I was privileged to lecture on the future of ALPB at its centennial celebration. I continue to work with this worthy organization. Indeed, it has published this memoir.

DENOUEMENT

Returning to Roanoke College.... That golden age of Christian teaching and intellectual production (2000-2015) gradually faded, however. Soon after 2010 a new curriculum supplanted the old one that had a required course in religion and philosophy. Called "Inquiry" (INQ), the new curriculum reverted to a "distribution" system in which students have a wide variety of choices among highly specific course offerings. It is no longer "content based." The stated purposes of Roanoke College no longer insist that an educated person should engage fields of important knowledge and wisdom. No Christian-oriented courses are required among the choices. Rather, the college claims that each course must inculcate a "way of thinking" that will encourage responsible decisions and actions. But there is little overtly "Christian" about that "way of thinking." In fact, such an approach may be more corrosive than supportive of any robust tradition. In spite of the gains enumerated above and the efforts that were made toward making the Lutheran/Christian heritage of the college more publicly relevant, the college as a whole has slowly moved away from that goal.

Indeed, the college seems quite bashful about presenting itself as a college in which the Christian heritage is honored. New faculty are not expected to support that part of the college mission that "honors its Christian heritage and partnership with the Lutheran church by nurturing a dialog between faith and reason." About a half dozen Lutherans are left on the faculty. The vast majority of the faculty are unaware of or apathetic toward its Christian heritage. The Religion and Philosophy Department—in spite of its four endowed chairs in Christian studies—is increasingly dominated by "religious studies" advocates, who believe that the department should not advance the cause of the Christian faith but rather study about it "objectively," along with other religions. One strong Christian professor—Gerald McDermott—left for Beeson Divinity School in 2015 while more "religious studies" types were brought on.

At my retirement from administering the Center for Religion and Society in 2012, I was made a "research associate," a title that gave me staff status and an office. Since the Religion and Philosophy Department was fully staffed by then, there was little opportunity for me to continue as an adjunct professor. However, I was invited by a new online seminary, the Institute of Lutheran Theology, to join its faculty. From then on I have taught one course a term for the seminary: Christian ethics in the fall and Christian sexual ethics in the spring, and, sometimes during the summer, a course in Theological Interpretation of Film. Most of the students are adults who have experienced a call to the ordained ministry. I find the work quite congenial.

I have continued to write editorials and essays for a variety of newspapers and journals, and continue to lecture, especially on Christian higher education. But my main project from 2012 on was to write a history of the college, particularly focusing on its relation to its Christian heritage. I worked through the eras of each of the ten presidents of the college, examining their vision of the college in relation to the college identity and mission that was already extant. I also researched the curricula, the ethos, and faculty profile for each presidential era. There were many surprises: that the founder, David Bittle, was a fiery evangelical with little Lutheran theological substance; that the college was deeply committed to the "Christian republican" project to form young men in Christian virtue for the sake of the young republic and the church; and that a specifically Lutheran identity did not emerge until the tenure of Norman Fintel from 1975 to 1989.

In the chapter on Fintel, I note how he made a strong effort to strengthen the Lutheran/Christian character of the college, including hiring me for a newly endowed chair in religion—the Jordan Trexler—as well as pursuing other wealthy Lutheran donors for three more endowed chairs. He also raised money for a Center for Religion and Society, which I organized and ran for thirty years. He worked for an endowment for the Lutheran chaplaincy, recruited a strong

Christian choir director, brought the Virginia Synod headquarters onto campus, and hired an academic dean—Gerald Gibson—who was supportive of the Christian heritage of the college. These were major gains in strengthening the public relevance of the Lutheran/Christian heritage.

Following the book's Fintel chapter, I then traced how the succeeding presidents cultivated the gains that he had made. But as time passed, it became clear that there was little desire among them to press beyond Fintel's robust agenda, especially before a faculty that was not particularly friendly to it. Roanoke reverted to its habit of pragmatically adapting to the dominant academic culture. When it was evangelical early on it operated out of that perspective for fifty years, when mainline Protestant, out of that. Its brief Lutheran flurry has been slowly marginalized by the reigning "secular progressive" academic culture. The public relevance of its religious heritage has faded in response to a culture that renders religion publicly invisible. The ideology of "inclusion and diversity" has come to dominate. The college carefully notes how many African-Americans are on the faculty, but doesn't keep track of the number of Lutherans.

In the last chapter of that book I projected two possible scenarios of the college's future: one in which intentional steps were taken by the leadership of the college to preserve the public relevance of its religious heritage (the glass is half full) and one in which the gradual marginalization of that heritage would ensue, finally rendering it irrelevant in any public way (the glass is empty.) I meant it as a summons to our college leadership to take up the strategy I commended.

The Eerdmans company, which had published three other of my books, brought it out in the fall of 2017. The title we settled on was: *Keeping the Soul in Christian Higher Education: A History of Roanoke College*. We wanted a title directed at a larger readership than just Roanoke's. I wrote it to make Roanoke's history and prospects a model for other church-related colleges and universities of a similar type. My hope was that the last chapter would provide similar schools a strategy for preserving and perhaps even strengthening their "soul." Since its publication it has garnered some appreciative reviews and a number of invitations for me to speak at Christian schools.

I am very glad I pitched the book to a larger readership than Roanoke's, because it has not stirred much discussion at Roanoke, to my great disappointment. I timed its appearance to coincide with the 175th anniversary of the college and the 500th anniversary of the Reformation, two major occasions for the college to reflect on its identity and mission as a Lutheran-related college. I thought my book would be part of a wider college conversation on those important subjects. In the run-up to 2017-18, I talked expectantly with President Maxey and Chaplain Bowen about various ways such a conversation could take place, and encouraged them to take up the task with vigor. I especially urged the president to lead the discussion. He seemed to be interested in taking up the cause; he even invited me to engage the board of the college in a serious discussion of the college mission. Sadly, nothing happened. No discussion, no college-wide program, no mention of my book. Even my invitation to speak to the board was reduced from a serious encounter to a five minute talk before the board dinner. It was clear that the leadership—including Lutherans on the board—wanted no such conversation.

The serious Christians—of a classical sort—on the faculty are dispirited. They keep their convictions private. The board is not alert enough to the secularist threat to be dispirited or alarmed. The administration has other projects on its mind. No one in the college cares enough about "keeping its soul" to press the cause. I'm afraid the "game is over." I'm resigned to experience, and maybe even enjoy, Roanoke College as the secular school it is becoming. There will still be many fine Christians on campus, but their presence will be below the surface, as it is in a myriad of secular schools.

THE ERA OF CHURCH STRIFE AND NEW BEGINNINGS

In chapter two I recounted our (Joanna's and my) involvement in local parish life, which led in 2015 to our departure from College Lutheran Church (Evangelical Lutheran Church in America) after thirty-three years in order to move to St. John Lutheran Church (North American Lutheran Church). This was spurred by the ELCA's full embrace of gay marriage and partnered gay pastors in 2009. Though College Lutheran was certainly not in harmony with those moves by the national church, it was becoming impossible for us to stay in a local parish affiliated with the ELCA. Our ecclesiological commitments take seriously what happens at the national level. We do not want to belong to a church that had departs from orthodox Christian teaching on sexuality, one that even uncritically embraces transgenderism.

There is a whole history of intellectual engagement on those issues that I did not elaborate in that chapter. So here goes....

As I mentioned in the chapter on the church, the 60s (1965-75) had powerful effects on the Lutheran Church in America (1962-1987), the church to which we belonged after the merger of the United Lutheran Church in America and a number of ethnically-based Lutheran churches. But those effects were gradual; it took quite a time for the feminist, multiculturalist, and gay liberation movements to enact "their long march through the institutions," as Rudi Duetschke, the German student revolutionary, had anticipated. But march they did.

Since I still had the aura of a liberal in the early 70s, I was appointed to the LCA's Task Force on Women and Men in Church and Society in that era. The task force was dominated by a group of militant feminists who pushed strongly for more women pastors in the church and women's equality in society, both goals with which I agreed. They also began pressing for more "inclusive" language in worship. Several suggested to the committee producing a new hymnal that the wedding vows should be changed from "until death do us part" to "until love ends." They were strongly "pro-choice." Several were lesbians intent on changing the church's teaching and practice on homosexuality. They were the vanguard of the future.

Since I was moving toward a more conservative stance on sexuality issues by the mid-70s, the meetings were absolutely painful. I was pretty much out of harmony with their sexuality agenda and was thankful when the Task Force concluded. I remember my contribution to our last meeting. I warned that the task force had demoted the roles of wife and mother in its headlong affirmation of women's movement into the economy. I was actually "defending" my wife, Joanna, who was beginning to feel beleaguered as a "stay-at-home mom" in the very liberal neighborhood of Hyde Park, Chicago.

As I recounted in the chapter on the church, the radicalized leaders of the liberationist movements gained more and more traction throughout the 80s, especially with feminist-oriented women pastors and black and ethnic minority activists pushing hard. By the time that the new church—the Evangelical Lutheran Church in America—was organized in the late 80s, the activists had driven the virus of identity politics and its attendant quotas deep into its institutional make-up. The words "inclusivity" and "diversity" became the "god words" that trumped all other objectives. Ironically, the new church was "ahead of the curve" compared to their use in the larger society. Quotas guaranteed that all committees of the church were at least half women and ten percent "people of color or whose language was other than English." The quota system also shaped the new ELCA's burgeoning bureaucracies—Women, Multicultural, Ministry, Youth, Church and Society, Outreach, and Global Missions. Possessing theological acumen was not a requirement. Those divisions and commissions of the church pushed the liberationist agenda relentlessly as the years went by. A strong outside, lavishly-funded, gay organization, Lutherans Concerned, carried on an organized campaign that successfully persuaded many congregations and institutions of the church to become "Reconciled in Christ." Under the guise of that traditional slogan Lutherans Concerned brought its whole agenda of morally legitimating homosexual conduct, and, in the long run, of getting the church to accept gay marriage and partnered gay pastors.

In 1992 the Division for Church and Society, chaired by a vigorous feminist, who earlier had in 1982 succeeded me in the church and society chair at LSTC, released a sexuality statement that was way ahead of where the rank-and-file of the church were. On the day of its release I was speaking at Concordia Seminary in St. Louis and the leading St. Louis newspaper trumpeted: "ELCA Endorses Masturbation." A bit embarrassing. After the statement was retracted, a task force of about twenty was appointed to ponder how the church should proceed on these sexuality issues. The task force decided that each member should take responsibility to hold a constructive dialog on these issues in their own bailiwick. I organized a "Disputation on Homosexuality" at Roanoke College that featured a debate between a revisionist Lutheran professor (Paul Jersild) and an orthodox Lutheran theological ethicist (Gilbert Meilaender), followed by a panel discussion that featured several bishops and pastors. I even invited the director of Lutherans Concerned to be part of the panel. The excellent papers given by the theologians were widely distributed in the church. I still use them in my classes on sexual ethics.

However, when the task force gathered to report on their efforts, I found that mine was the only one that gave voice to the traditional teachings on homosexuality. All the rest were partisan efforts to persuade their audiences to the revisionist position. To my chagrin I found that I was the only one on the task force to support the traditional teaching. The chairman of the Council of Bishops was completely silent during the meetings, but after the final meeting I saw him consulting with the gay activists on the task force. Later I found the same imbalance to be true among the annual gathering of Lutheran ethicists, as well as of the official ELCA task force charged to write a new social statement on sexuality. The handwriting was on the wall.

Multiculturalists, ethnic minority activists, and feminists gradually introduced a perspectivalist agenda into the theological reflection of the church. One's identity constituted one's theological clout. A plethora of "genitive theologies" ("theologies of") emerged—feminist, black, Latino, gay, and multicultural. The ELCA's traditional theologians were marginalized, as were its bishops, who were almost exclusively white male at the beginning of the church. Right when the new church needed a steady theological guidance system there was only chaos and confusion. That offered an open door to the machinations of the bureaucracy.

In the 90s anti-colonialists in the Division for Global Mission rejected "pioneer evangelism" (bringing the gospel to those who had never heard it) for "accompaniment" (working with already established churches). They believed the former was too contaminated by colonialism to be viable and faithful. Many pioneer evangelism societies—to the Chinese, Muslims, Africans—were "orphaned" and had to go it on their own, without support from the national church. So much for the Great Commission.

The feminists in the bureaucracy made sure that the ELCA never became an advocate for pro-life causes in church or society. Not even a whisper. The church's earlier ministries to political actors at the state and national levels became "advocacy" offices which took partisan positions on many issues, almost always coinciding with the liberal political agenda.

These efforts were slowly drawing the ELCA into a declining liberal Protestantism, along with the Episcopalians, Presbyterians, United Church of Christ, and Methodists. Oddly though, organized resistance to the liberationist agenda was late in coming in the ELCA. Other mainline denominations had spawned more and earlier protest organizations, though, in true Lutheran fashion, two large theological gatherings—entitled "Called to

Faithfulness"—were held at St. Olaf College in the early 90s to sound the alarm about the direction of the new church. *Dialog*, a feisty theological journal edited by Carl Braaten and Robert Jenson, offered a running critical commentary on the run-up to the new church as well as its early days. I wrote a number of articles in that series, one entitled "Merging into the Mainstream." All three Lutheran independent journals—*Dialog, Lutheran Quarterly, Lutheran Forum*—were highly critical of developments in the new church. Other protest gatherings were held, several at which I spoke.

The first organized resistance in the ELCA—Word Alone—formed about the turn of the century. It gathered in protest of the ELCA's new requirement for Lutheran ordinations, i.e., that they were only valid if a bishop in the apostolic succession were present. That requirement was a part of the agreement made with the Episcopal Church entitled *Called to Common Mission*. It generated much heat among low-church Lutherans of the Midwest. I could not get that excited about that particular issue, though I voted against the agreement when it came up on the agenda of the Virginia Synod Assembly. Given the state of Episcopal bishops—a heretical John Shelby Spong, an openly gay bishop Gene Robinson—I thought it unwise to make any agreement with the Episcopal Church at that time.

Word Alone organized as an association of Lutheran churches—not a church—and provided a landing place for hundreds of churches that were fed up and wanted out of the ELCA. Word Alone also helped form another group—Solid Rock—that was much more disturbed than Word Alone itself about the effects of all the liberationist movements mentioned above, but especially about the slow march toward acceptance of gay marriage and the ordination of partnered gays. A former ELCA bishop, Paull Spring, pastors of several large churches, and a number of dissident clergy and layfolks (including me) met at Luther Seminary in 2003 to organize resistance to the coming efforts at the 2005 ELCA Churchwide Assembly to bless gay unions and ordain partnered gays. A network of solidly orthodox clergy and laity was organized to garner enough support successfully to fend off those initiatives. Our main effort focused on getting orthodox Lutherans elected as delegates. I was part of Solid Rock's actions before the 2005 Assembly, and was elected as a voting delegate to the Assembly. We were able to block the revisionist agenda at that point.

The leaders of the ELCA, after so much turbulence, pledged that the Churchwide Assembly of 2007 would not deal with those issues, so we in Solid Rock did not organize resistance at that assembly. Shockingly however, one bishop introduced a motion—that carried—at the very end of the assembly that called upon bishops not to discipline any clergy who were irregularly ordained or who were performing blessings of gay unions. That move, of course, pushed the progressive cause further, which was to achieve a great victory for heresy in the assembly of 2009.

We decided to change the name of Solid Rock—a one issue organization—to CORE (Coalition for Reform)—an organization with a larger scope. The new organization needed full-time leadership, so we asked Roy Harrisville III to be its convener. He consented and led the effort to strengthen and broaden the network of resistance. We wrote and organized, but to no avail. The contested two initiatives—to bless gay unions and to allow partnered gays—needed only a simple majority of votes and they passed handily. The incredibly ambivalent social statement on sexuality issues—*Sexuality: Gift and Trust*—needed a two thirds majority and it got it by one vote. The winning number was 666 and the vote was accompanied by a rogue tornado in Minneapolis that halted the assembly and blew the cross off a nearby Lutheran church. The resistors, of course, thought this was a word from God while the revisionists noted that the sun came out after the storm.

I actually felt a huge sense of relief after we were beaten on all three contested initiatives. We knew support for CORE would dry up after the defeat and no one among the CORE leadership had any desire to continue to work for reform inside the ELCA. Personally, the defeat meant the end of nearly twenty years of "rear guard" efforts to try to stop the inevitable march to liberal Protestantism by the ELCA. I didn't have to struggle any more. I was free.

But what to do next? Answering that question was more than an individual matter. So the leadership of CORE—changed now to Coalition for Renewal—decided to meet in the Indianapolis area in the fall of 2009 to decide what to do. We planned to meet in a large Lutheran church but there were so many who wanted to attend that we had to move to a much larger Catholic church in Fishers, Indiana. The sessions were electric. (At the concluding Eucharist I received the Bread from the Rev. Paul Krebs, my dear friend of many years and the son of my confirmation pastor, George Krebs, pastor of Grace Lutheran in West Point, Nebraska. It was a powerful experience.) There was no doubt about what should be done. A new Lutheran church should be formed in 2010 that would be more faithful to orthodox Christianity and to the Lutheran Confessions. One of the convictions that emerged was that a new church should be much more serious than the ELCA about theology and its role in the church.

On behalf of CORE, then, Carl Braaten and I organized a theological conference that would precede the founding of the new church in August, 2010. It was the first major gathering after Fisher's. It's theme was "Seeking New Directions for Lutheranism" and was held at the large Upper Arlington Lutheran Church in suburban Columbus, Ohio. Carl and I invited quite a distinguished set of guests to lecture: Robert Jenson, Steven Paulson, Paul Martinson, Stephen Hultgren, Frank Senn, and Paul Hinlicky. He and I also lectured.

When I rose to introduce the first theological lecturer, I was astounded as I turned to the assembly in the huge nave. Nearly one thousand people were jammed into the church! They were there to hear the theological rationale for a new beginning in

American Lutheranism, The North American Lutheran Church. And they were there at their own initiative and expense. I lectured on "Renewing the Moral Vision for Lutheranism," which was a critique of what the ELCA had done as well as a summons to recover the biblical and traditional grounds for doing Christian ethics. The lectures, edited by Carl, were later published by the American Lutheran Publicity Bureau. The book sold briskly.

After that exhilarating theological conference, the crowd journeyed to an enormous Nazarene church in a southern suburb of Columbus where the new church was founded and its new leader, Bishop Paull Spring, was installed. Paull had been the leader and mainstay of the movement toward new beginnings since our first meeting at Luther Seminary in 2003. Over the months after the August founding, a new Lutheran church was organized. Many ELCA churches joined. I was asked to be on its Commission for Theology and Doctrine, on which I still serve.

After the great success of the first CORE theological conference, Carl and I organized four more: a second at Upper Arlington on "No Other Name;" a third in the Minneapolis area on "Teaching and Preaching the Law and Gospel of God;" a fourth in Pittsburgh on "Being the Church in These Perilous Times:" and a fifth in Charleston, SC, on "Rightly Handling the Word of Truth." Each set of lectures was edited by Carl and published by the ALPB. After the fifth year we passed the task of organizing the lectures to a committee of Lutheran theologians. The series continues to the present time under the auspices of the North American Lutheran Church. Happily for us, the church named the theological lectures in our honor in 2016: The Braaten-Benne Theological Lectures.

In 2011 Carl and I also organized a Young Theologians Group that met for two days prior to the theological lectures. We thought that the new North American Lutheran Church would need a supply of younger theologians to take over from the older ones who made up its Commission on Theology and

Doctrine. About twenty were gathered into yearly meetings and at least three of those "incubated" in the group are now on the Commission. The group continues under the leadership of Nathan Yoder, who participated in the very first young theologians' gathering.

Though church schisms are undoubtedly serious matters that should be undertaken with trepidation, it has seemed clear to me that the schismatic party was actually the ELCA. It simply collapsed before "progressive" American culture, as did other mainline Protestant denominations, who also experienced schisms. The ELCA bishops, whose first duty was to defend the orthodox faith, failed miserably. Not one led a synod that resisted the drift to heresy. Thus, the church departed from orthodox teachings on evangelism and marriage, though the underlying issue was the denial of the authority of the Bible and the Great Tradition on these matters.

The North American Lutheran Church has been a great refreshment to me, at both the local and national levels. St. John in Roanoke is a vibrant Lutheran church—liturgical, sacramental, orthodox, missional—that has honored me with an official role as teacher of the church. The national church is led by trustworthy leaders and enjoys a faithful clergy and laity. I have had a role in its formation and ongoing life, especially its commitment to orthodox Lutheran ethics. It is small—about 450 congregations—but growing, so we hope and pray for its prospects.

I enjoy teaching Christian ethics at an online seminary, The Institute of Lutheran Theology, and have confidence that my engagement with its many adult seminarians is fruitful for their ministries. My continued participation in the board of the American Lutheran Publicity Bureau provides an additional opportunity to enjoy and promote the Lutheranism I have loved for a lifetime.

CONCLUDING THOUGHTS

As I look back over fifty-five years of teaching, lecturing, and writing, I think the churchly role I have sketched immediately above is one that has had discernable effects. For many years I participated in efforts by theologians—clergy and lay—to resist the movement of the ELCA to liberal Protestantism. Those efforts impeded the church for a time but finally came to naught. So we participated in "new beginnings" after 2009. Those efforts have helped to form—we hope with the Spirit's guidance—a church that hues to authentically Lutheran teachings and practices.

A second area in which my work has had noticeable effects is in the field of Christian higher education, though, ironically, I have been unable to staunch the tides of secularization in my own college. But my book, *Quality with Soul*, my many essays and articles, and especially my numerous lectures and consultations with Christian colleges and universities have left a discernable mark. Administrators and faculty of those schools have taken the time to witness to my work, for which I am very grateful. My "students" have carried on the mission of Christian higher education in many schools.

As to my own school, Roanoke College, I take satisfaction in having participated in a brief period of strengthened public relevance of the Lutheran/Christian heritage of the school. I was a partner in the efforts of Norman Fintel to strengthen the connection between the college and the Lutheran church and its heritage. Many others, of course, pitched in. But since the college has rarely (except perhaps for its first fifty years) had a clear enough sense of mission to "hire for that mission" in its religious dimension, it has been dependent on the reigning culture of higher education, which, for its early years was evangelical, and for its later years was a kind of generic American Protestantism. As that academic culture has become more indifferent and, in many ways, hostile, to the role of Christianity in higher education, the college has slowly succumbed to its secularizing pressures, as have almost all mainline colleges. Their sponsoring traditions are at most grace notes or historical markers for them, with little public relevance for the things that matter. However, I continue to enjoy Roanoke as a good liberal arts college in a lovely part of the country in which a discerning student can find still some excellent Christian teaching and counseling. My own granddaughter benefited immensely from such opportunities. The college has been good to me and I think I have played my part, though fleeting, in contributing to its religious educational mission.

Less measureable effects have accrued to my work in Christian ethics in their Lutheran construal. I have taught, written, and lectured for over a half-century about the Christian life in the light of the Lutheran doctrine of vocation. I have done likewise with my Lutheran "take" on the role of religion in political, social, and economic life. I have taught thousands of students in hundreds of courses in my fifty-five years as a faculty member of two seminaries and a college. I have lectured at over 120 colleges, universities, and seminaries. I have written hundreds of shorter pieces on Christian perspectives on an array of topics in church and society. One simply doesn't know whether or how much those efforts have edified students and readers. Now and then a blessed soul will come forth to tell me how much they appreciated *Ordinary Saints* or *The Paradoxical Vision*. Or I will get a letter or e-mail in praise of one of my writings. However, those experiences are not everyday occurrences. I, like everyone else, must live in hope that our sovereign Lord has found some of our contributions useful to his work in the church and the world.

Far better than praise have been the many friendships I have found over the years of my work in Christian higher education, new directions in Lutheranism, and practical theological engagement with many issues and causes. Those friendships have "filled my cup of being" with the needed support and encouragement to persist. They have truly been precious. Added to those are the friendships of those involved in other callings—family, citizenship, and church. My cup runneth over.

This assessment of my life's work cannot be complete without mentioning a sense of my own sin and finitude. I am enough of a Lutheran to believe that both the motives and the effects of my work are highly mixed. No doubt I have been tempted toward an inflated sense that my judgments are true, and a disdain for those held by my opponents. I certainly took that posture when I was deeply involved in the idealistic liberalism of the early 60s. My focus on the church as primarily an instrument of social transformation is something I deeply regret. My only excuse is that I changed direction when the full implications of what I was teaching became clear. Further, I have a competitive spirit that sometimes drives me to fight for my side, with only a casual thought about whether or not I have the right on my side. I know that often my knowledge has been limited by my own sloth and distorted by my own carelessness. Nevertheless, I have had the courage—or foolhardiness—to "sin boldly." Lord have mercy.

I am aware enough that my effects on the world are so obscure and passing that sometimes I am tempted to despair. In the big picture, what I have done is infinitely small and negligible. Or, if I have had an effect, it might be negative rather than positive. Such reflections lead me to reliance on the mercy and grace of God in Christ for forgiveness for my sinful self's waywardness. Kierkegaard once opined that "it is a comforting thought to know that before God we are always wrong." Such an awareness leads to repentance and a longing for forgiveness. It also leads one to a quiet confidence that one's eternal destiny is not dependent upon one's work, but on one's trust in the love of God in Christ. The Lord is my Shepherd.

As to my earthly destiny, that calling by the Spirit to serve Christ's church so many years ago took a different route than I had expected. I thought I was called to the ordained ministry, but it turned out that I was called to be a teacher in the church, specializing in Christian ethics. I dearly hope and pray that I have been useful to the Lord. But if he doesn't use my offerings, what matter. His will prevails with or without me; he is the Sovereign One. Yet, I have consented to his call and found intrinsic meaning and joy in the work to which he called me. Thanks be to God!

WRITINGS

BOOKS

Wandering in the Wilderness: Christians and the New Culture. Philadelphia: Fortress Press, 1972.

Defining America: A Christian Critique of the American Dream. Philadelphia: Fortress Press, 1974. (Jointly authored with Philip Hefner)

The Ethic of Democratic Capitalism: A Moral Reassessment. Philadelphia: Fortress Press, 1981.

Ordinary Saints: An Introduction to the Christian Life. Philadelphia: Fortress Press, first edition 1988; second edition Minneapolis: Fortress Press, 2003.

The Paradoxical Vision: A Public Theology for the Twenty-first Century. Minneapolis: Fortress Press, 1995.

Seeing is Believing: Visions of Life Through Film. Lanham, MD: University Press of America, 1998.

Why Bother? A Whole Vision for a Whole People. Minneapolis: Augsburg Fortress, 1999.

Quality with Soul: How Six Premier Colleges and Universities Keep Faith with Their Religious Traditions. Grand Rapids: Wm. B. Eerdmans Publishing Co., 2001.

Reasonable Ethics: A Christian Approach to Social, Economic, and Political Concerns. St. Louis: Concordia Publishing House, 2005.

A Report from the Front Lines: A Festschrift in Honor of Robert Benne. Introduced and edited by Michael Shahan. Grand Rapids: Wm. B. Eerdmans Publishing Co., 2009.

Good and Bad Ways to Think About Religion and Politics. Grand Rapids: Wm. B. Eerdmans Publishing Co., 2010.

Die Paradoxe Vision: Eine Offentliche Theologie fur das 21. Jahrhundert, Leipzig: Evangelische Verlagsanstalt Gmbh, 2015. A German Translation (abridged) of *Paradoxical Vision: A Public Theology for the Twenty-first Century.* Minneapolis: Fortress Press, 1995.

Keeping the Soul in Christian Higher Education: A History of Roanoke College. Grand Rapids: Wm. B. Eerdmans Publishing Co. 2017.

Thanks Be to God: Memoirs of a Practical Theologian. Delhi, NY: American Lutheran Publicity Bureau, 2019.

CHAPTERS IN BOOKS

"The Impact of the Future" in *The Shaping of the Parish for the Future*, ed. Gilbert (Philadelphia: Parish Life Press, 1975), 1-26.

"Values, Technology, and the American Future; a Comparative Analysis of Robert Heilbroner and Daniel Bell" in *Belonging and Alienation: Religious Foundations for the Human Future*, ed. Hefner and Schroeder (Chicago: Chicago Center for the Scientific Study of Religion, 1976), 95-125.

"Searching for the Switchman" in *Belief and Ethics: Essays in Ethics, the Human Sciences, and Ministry in Honor of W. Alvin Pitcher*, ed. Schroeder and Winter (Chicago: Center for the Scientific Study of Religion, 1978), 129-139.

"The Social Sources of Church Polity" in *The New Church Debate: Issues Facing American Lutheranism*, ed. Braaten (Philadelphia: Fortress Press, 1983), 169-183.

"A Democratic Capitalist Approach to Regulation" in *Regulatory Reform: New Vision or Old Curse*, ed. Kuhn and Maxey (New York: Praeger Publishers, 1985), 159-177.

"Capitalism with Fewer Tears" in *Christianity and Capitalism: Perspectives on Religion, Liberalism, and the Economy*, ed. Grelle and Krueger (Chicago: Center for the Scientific Study of Religion, 1986), 67-79.

"Comment on Gregory Baum's Interpretation of Recent Catholic Social Teaching" in *Religion, Economics, and Social Thought: Proceedings of an International Symposium*, ed. Block and Hexham (Vancouver BC: Fraser Institute, 1986), 72-82.

"Two Cheers for the Bishops" in *God, Goods, and the Common God*, ed. Lutz (Minneapolis: Augsburg Publishing House, 1987), 45-61.

"The Bishops' Letter: A Protestant Reading" in *The Catholic Challenge to the American Economy: Reflections on the U.S. Bishops' Pastoral Letter on Catholic Social Teaching and the U.S. Economy*, ed. Gannon (New York: Macmillan Publishing Co., 1987), 76-86.

"Religion and Politics: Four Possible Connections" in *Discourse and the Two Cultures: Science, Religion and the Humanities*, ed. Thompson (Lanham, MD: University Press of America, 1988), 231-263.

"The Preferential Option for the Poor and American Public Policy" in *The Preferential Option for the Poor*, ed. Neuhaus (Grand Rapids: Wm. B. Eerdmans Publishing Co., 1988), 53-72.

"Reformed Capitalism or Aristocratic Socialism? A Response to Franklin Gamwell" in *Economic Life*, ed. Gamwell and Schroeder (Chicago: Center for the Scientific Study of Religion, 1988), 251-259.

"John Paul II's Challenge to Democratic Capitalism" in *The Making of an Economic Vision*, ed. Houck and Williams (Lanham, MD: University Press of America, 1991), 121-139.

"A Response to a Post-communist Manifesto" in *From Christ to the World: Introductory Readings in Christian Ethics*, ed. Boulton, Kennedy, and Verhey (Grand Rapids: Wm. B. Eerdmans Publishing Co., 1994), 489-493.

"A Flagging Flagship?" in *Called to Serve: St. Olaf and the Vocation of a Church College*, ed. Schwandt (Northfield: St. Olaf College Press, 1999), 231-239.

"A Lutheran Vision of Christian Humanism" in *Christ and Culture in Dialogue*, ed. Menuge (St. Louis: Concordia Academic Press, 1999), 314-332.

"The Case of the Forgotten Fifth: Response to Carl Braaten" in *Being Christian Today*, ed. Neuhaus and Weigel (Washington: Ethics and Public Policy Center, 1992), 122-126.

"Green Shoots in America: Religion and the Renewal of Culture" in *Public Life and the Renewal of Culture*, ed. Box and Quinlivan (Latrobe: Center for Economic and Policy Education, 1996), 25-35.

"The Calling of the Church in Economic Life" in *The Two Cities of God: The Church's Responsibility for the Earthly City*, ed. Braaten and Jenson (Grand Rapids: Wm. B. Eerdmans Publishing Co., 1997), 95-117.

"The Church and Politics: Hot and Cool Connections" in *Moral Issues and Christian Response: Sixth Edition*, ed. Jersild and Jung (Fort Worth: Harcourt Brace College Publishers, 1998), 10-17.

"Lutheran Ethics: Perennial Themes and Contemporary Challenges" in *The Promise of Lutheran Ethics*, ed. Bloomquist and Stumme (Minneapolis: Fortress, 1998), 11-31.

"Integrity and Fragmentation: Can the Lutheran Center Hold?" in *Lutherans Today: American Lutheran Identity in the Twenty-first Century*, ed. Cimono (Grand Rapids: Wm. B. Eerdmans Publishing Company, 2003), 206-222.

"Christians and Government" in *The Oxford Handbook of Theological Ethics*, ed. Meilaender and Werpehowski (New York: Oxford University Press, 2005), 325-343.

"The Lutheran Vision: a Theological Framework for Social Ethics" in *Ritrod: Gudfradistofnunar Tileinkud Dr. Birni Bjornssyni Sjotugum* (A Festschrift for Dr. Bjorn Bjornsson), ed. Boasdottir, Jonsson, and Petursson (Gudfradistofnun: Skalholtsutgafan, 2007), 35-49.

"Authority and Power in the ELCA" in *By What Authority: Confronting Churches Who No Longer Believe Their Own Message*, ed. Egland, (Hoffman: Hoffman House Press, 2008), 43-53.

"Renewing the Moral Vision for Lutheranism" in *Seeking New Directions for Lutheranism: Biblical, Theological, and Churchly Perspectives*, ed. Braaten (Delhi: ALPB Books, 2010), 155-171.

"Engaging in Politics: Yes; Politicizing the Church: No" in *No Other Name: Salvation Through Christ Alone*, ed. Braaten (Delhi: ALPB Books, 2012), 53-71.

"Church-related Colleges and Universities" (291-292) and "The Secularization of Christian Colleges and Universities" (1130-1131), in *Encyclopedia of Christian Education*, ed. Kurian and Lamport (Lanham, MD: Rowman and Littlefield, 2015).

"The Lutheran Paradoxical View" in *Five Visions of Church and Politics*, ed. Black and Gundry (Grand Rapids: Zondervan, 2015), 59-97.

"How Should Modern Lutherans Try to Shape Secular Law" in *Human Governance: Lutheran Perspectives on Contemporary Legal Issues*, ed. Duty and Failinger (Grand Rapids: Wm. Eerdmans Publishing Co., 2016), 328-340.

"Theology and Politics: Reinhold Niebuhr's Christian Zionism" in *The New Christian Zionism: Fresh Perspectives on Israel and the Land*, ed. McDermott (Downers Grove: InterVarsity Press, 2016), 198-221.

"Identity and Fragmentation: Can the Lutheran Center Hold?" in *The Vocation of Lutheran Higher Education*, ed. Jason Mahn (Minneapolis: Lutheran University Press, 2017), 158-171.

"Economic Issues: Capitalism and Socialism" 204-205, "Economic Life and Lutheranism" 205-206, "Priesthood of All Believers" 620-621, and "State" 701-704, in *Dictionary of Luther and the Lutheran Traditions*, ed. Wengert (Grand Rapids: Baker Academic, 2017).

"Luther's Teaching on the Vocations of Christians" in *The Oxford Research Encyclopedia of Martin Luther*, ed. Hinlicky and Nelson (New York: Oxford Books, 2017).

INDEX OF NAMES

A
Albee, Edward, 129
Althaus, Paul, 102
Andersen, Harry, 49
Alinsky, Saul, 83, 109
Almy, Amy, 37
Amlinger, Lore, 129
Arendt, Hannah, 107, 111
Aulen, Gustaf, 104

B
Bahe, Al, 75
Bansemer, Richard, 35, 57
Barth, Karl, 48, 49, 102, 103, 105
Barth, Markus, 105
Beckenhauer, Blanche, 39
Becker, Larry, 45
Bell, Daniel, 112
Bellah, Robert, 94, 130
Benne, Alex, 18, 30, 57
Benne, Andrew, 18, 30, 35, 57
Benne, Brad, 25
Benne, Caroline Johnson, 30
Benne, Chris, 25
Benne, Dallas, 15, 18, 19, 22, 24, 25, 28, 29, 32, 42, 71, 72, 73, 76, 92, 93
Benne, David, 25
Benne, Elizabeth, 18, 30
Benne, Ian, 18, 30
Benne, Irene Classen, 15, 18, 19, 24, 28, 29, 32, 72, 73, 74
Benne, Joanna Carson, 7, 16, 17, 18, 26, 45, 47, 48, 57, 59, 62, 63, 79, 80, 81, 121, 159, 160
Benne, Johann Friederich, 22, 23
Benne, Johann Heinrich, 23
Benne, John, 32
Benne, Herman, 14, 22
Benne, Jack, 22
Benne, John, 14, 22, 23
Benne, Kenneth, 15, 21, 25, 29, 72
Benne, Max, 18, 30, 57
Benne, Michael, 17, 27, 28, 30, 35, 36, 53, 57
Benne, Nicholas, 17, 27, 28, 57
Benne, Pat Richmond, 25, 29
Benne, Philip, 17, 26, 28, 34, 50
Benne, Pauline Poledna, 14
Benne, Robert, 9, 15, 16, 17, 18
Benne, Stephanie Lundy, 30
Bernhardt, Carl, 39, 40
Bernhardt, Ruth, 73
Bittle, David, 156
Blakely, Thomas, 131
Bonhoeffer, Dietrich, 126
Bowen, Chris, 158
Braaten, Carl, 99, 110, 126, 154, 163, 165, 166
Bradosky, John, 61
Brauer, Jerald, 84, 105
Bring, Ragnar, 103
Brown, Raymond, 13
Brunner, Emil, 103
Brunner, Peter, 102
Buchanan, Kathryn, 124, 152
Bultmann, Rudolph, 102, 103, 110
Burtchaell, James, 134, 141, 144, 145, 146

C
Carson, Ellen Larson, 26
Carson, Robert, 26
Christ, Jesus, 10, 12, 13, 37, 39, 41, 62, 89, 109, 126, 130, 138, 170
Christianson, Carol, 34
Christianson, Gerald, 34, 84, 85, 103
Classen, George, 14, 20, 21
Classen, Maggie, 22
Classen, Mary Punzel, 14, 20, 21
Classen, Timmien, 20
Cox, Duane, 75, 76
Cox, Harvey, 106
Crumley, James, 131

D
Deines, Dixie, 52
Deines, Rick, 35, 52, 53, 85, 107
Duetschke, Rudi, 159

E
Eisenberg, William, 134
Elshtain, Jean, 154
Erickson, Carol Benne, 15, 21, 25, 72
Erickson, Floyd, 25
Erickson, Kathryn, 25
Erickson, Steve, 25

F
Fama, Eugene, 111
Faudel, Gesela Horn, 81
Faudel, Jack, 81
Finney, Leon, 109
Fischer, Pat, 76
Fintel, "Jo," 121
Fintel, Norman, 29, 91, 120, 121, 122, 124, 125, 127, 128, 132, 133, 135, 148, 156, 157, 168
Forell, George, 84, 104, 117
Frahm, Minnie, 74

Friedman, Milton, 112
Fry, Franklin, 86
Furchert, Wilma, 74

G
Gailbraith, Kenneth, 112
Garber, Aaron, 57
Gibson, Bob, 78
Gibson, Gerald, 124, 133, 135, 157
Graham, Mark, 36, 60,61, 62
Gimmestad, Herman, 78
God, 10, 11, 13, 31, 63, 69, 89, 95, 102, 106, 109, 126, 137, 138, 164, 170
Gring, David, 133, 135, 146, 148, 150, 151
Grundvig, Nicolai, 49

H
Haight, Mark, 43
Hanna, Edwin, 75
Harrisville, Roy III, 164
Hartshorne, Charles, 103
Harrington, Michael, 83, 106
Hasebroock, Margaret, 9, 38, 39
Hasebroock, Robert, 9
Hauck, Alan, 46, 102
Hawkinson, Sarah, 45
Hefner, Philip, 26, 27, 34, 41, 49, 53, 79, 83, 88, 90, 104, 113, 128
Hefner, Neva White, 26, 34, 41
Hill, C. William, 129
Hinlicky, Paul, 125, 132, 146, 152, 154, 165
Hinlicky, Wynemah, 36, 58,59
Hixon, Myles, 62
Holy Spirit, 10, 13, 41, 53, 62, 85, 95, 109, 138, 168, 170, 171
Horn, Else, 81
Horn, Walter, 81
Hultgren, Stephen, 165

J
Jenson, Robert, 163, 165
Jersild, Paul, 161
Jones, Robert, 76

K
Kase, Carmen, 73
Kase, Joseph, 19
Kennedy, John, 83, 85
Kennedy, Robert, 87
Kierkegaard, Soren, 46, 102, 170
Kilpatrick, James, 129
King, Martin Luther, Jr., 83, 87
Kline, Gerald, 34
Klink, William, 19, 32, 38
Kotlar, Lillian, 39

Kornhauser, William, 111
Krebs, George, 38, 40, 165
Krebs, Paul, 165
Kremer, Christopher, 17, 28, 30
Kremer, Dylan, 18, 30, 57
Kremer, Linnea, 18, 28, 30, 169
Kremer, Kai, 18, 30
Kremer, Kristin Benne, 17, 27, 28, 30, 35, 50
Kristol, Irving, 90, 112
Kuenneth, Walter, 83, 102

L
Lazareth, William, 104
Lesher, William, 110
Lochmann, Milos, 126
London, Jack, 74
Lord, 11, 63, 95, 169, 170
Lucas, Herbert, 80
Lueninghoener, Gilbert, 45

M
Magary, Margaret, 74
Martinson, Paul, 165
Marty, Martin, 46, 129, 147
Marx, Karl, 112
Mattson, A.D., 84
Mattson, Karl, 84, 85
Mauney, James, 35, 57, 59
Mauer, Wilhelm, 102
McDermott, Gerald, 60, 61, 124, 125, 132, 152, 154, 155
McKeon, Richard, 135
Maxey, Michael, 158
Mead, Lawrence, 130
Meadows, Morris, 79
Meilaender, Gilbert, 154, 161
Mills, C. Wright, 111
Motley, Marion, 93
Moyer, Virgil, 57
Mozart, Wolfgang, 48

N
Naumann, Michael, 128
Nelson, James, 119
Neuhaus, Richard, 87, 90, 98, 112, 130, 146, 154
Niebuhr, H. Richard, 11, 110, 126
Niebuhr, Reinhold, 46, 83, 85, 92, 102, 103, 104, 106, 107
Noll, Mark, 137, 154
Novak, Michael, 90, 112, 115
Nygren, Anders, 103, 104

O
Obama, Barack, 130
O'Hara, Sabine, 151, 152
Osborne, Tom, 78

P
Pannenberg, Wolfhart, 128
Paulson, Steven, 165
Peerman, Dean, 46
Pelikan, Jaroslav, 48, 50
Peterson, James, 152
Pitcher, Alvin, 83, 84, 105, 106, 108, 114
Podhoretz, Norman, 90
Powers, Gary, 82

R
Raspberry, William, 130
Rawls, John, 115
Reimers, Evelyn Benne, 22
Reimers, Gladys Benne, 22, 32
Ritzen, Ralph, 43
Roberts, Preston, 139
Robinson, Gene, 163
Ross, Dorothy Benne, 22

S
Senn, Frank, 165
Scott, Nathan, 103
Schmidt, Helmut, 128
Schmeltekopf, Don, 142, 145, 154
Schroeder, Widick, 114
Schumann, Charles, 125, 152
Schumann, Helen, 152
Serling, Rod, 110
Shahan, Michael, 153
Sherman, Franklin, 27, 84, 86, 89, 118
Sittler, Joseph, 121
Sleeper, Freeman, 124, 125
Spong, John, 163
Sponheim, Paul, 104
Spring, Paull, 163, 166
Stoessel, Walter, 128
Strickler, Gerald, 44
Stumme, John, 154
Sullivan, Leon, 120
Swanson, Tim, 121

T
Terhune, A.P., 74
Thielicke, Helmut, 103, 113, 119
Thiemann, Ronald, 154
Tise, Sisters, 125, 152
Thompson, Delilah, 39
Tillich, Paul, 103, 110
Tredway, Thomas, 27
Trump, Donald, 95
Tuite, Marjorie, 109

V
Vennergrund, Ben, 49, 50
Vennergrund, Ella, 49

W
Warner, Lloyd, 111
Westermann, Dwayne, 35, 56, 57, 58
Whitehead, Alfred, 103
Wicken, Jeffrey, 128
Wiecher, William, 58, 59
Wieman, Henry, 103
Wilken, Robert, 104
Wilkie, Wendell, 20
Wingren, Gustaf, 104, 117
Winter, Gibson, 107, 111, 114
Wisnefske, Ned, 124, 152
Wogaman, Philip, 127
Wright, N. T., 98, 130

Y
Yoder, Nathan, 167
Younger, Tank, 93

Z
Zimmerman, William, 44
Zorn, Hans, 124

Made in the USA
Monee, IL
22 December 2021